P9-ASM-643

The Just Demands of the Poor

◆ *Marie Augusta Neal, S.N.D. deN.*

The Just Demands of the Poor

Essays in Socio-Theology

PAULIST PRESS
New York / Mahwah

The Publisher gratefully acknowledges use of three charts, "World Population Growth, 1900–2100," "Growth Through Time, 8000 B.C. to 2000
A.D.," and "Growth by Region, 1975 to 2000 A.D.," reproduced by permission of the Population Reference Bureau, Inc., Washington, D.C.

Copyright © 1987 by Marie Augusta Neal

All rights reserved. No part of this book may be reproduced or trans-
mitted in any form or by any means, electronic or mechanical, including
photocopying, recording, or by any information storage and retrieval
system without permission in writing from the publisher.

Library of Congress Cataloging-in-Publication Data

Neal, Marie Augusta.
    The just demands of the poor.

    Bibliography: p.
    1. Church and the poor.   2. Poor.   I. Title.
BV639.P6N43   1986   261.8'5   86-20511
ISBN 0-8091-2845-4 (pbk.)

Published by Paulist Press
997 Macarthur Boulevard
Mahwah, N.J. 07430

Printed and bound in the United States of America

Contents

Preface

In 1977 Paulist Press published a collection of some of my essays under the title *A Socio-Theology of Letting Go: The Role of a First World Church Facing Third World Peoples*. It was soon out of print and I was urged to update it rather than republish it. The essays in this volume are a sequel to that book. They pursue the same theme, focusing on the search for an effective response to the just demands of the organizing poor. This response is shaped by my having examined the biblical mandates in the context of the changing society of today's world. I say "society" rather than "societies" because we on this planet now constitute an inter-acting community. Since it is not yet a community in which power is shared, however, we often act against the interests of those least able, economically, to survive.

We have our reasons, reasons that make sense, given certain assumptions. Some of these assumptions are biological, referring to limitations supposedly inherent in our genes; some are psychological, harking back to our inner longings and imagination; some are philosophical, said to be rooted in our human nature; and yet others are social, economic, and political and have to do, more or less candidly, with self-interest.

But our reasons have to be measured against the Judaeo-Christian tradition, its call for justice and peace and, especially, its claim that altruism—the giving of one's life for the stranger in need—is made possible by Jesus' redeeming death and resurrection.

Historically, we have yielded repeatedly to self-interest, our doctrine of altruism swallowed up in righteous concern for our own progeny. Who it is that make up our progeny is one of the central questions raised in these essays, which challenge the assumptions of enlightened self-interest that form the basis for our institutional policy.

The essays raise the question of why, as world population begins to level off and there is developed a technology that could provide for all, we continue to arm ourselves as a means of guaranteeing access to resources presumed to be scarce. They challenge an economic system that leaves some people chronically unemployed and unable to pay for the goods they need, thereby necessitating limited production for want of consumers. They expose, too, those theories, especially religious notions of God, which serve to legitimate institutions that benefit the advantaged but cannot meet the needs of the world's peoples.

We have recently recognized the human rights of traditionally deprived peoples. I hope here to clarify the choices we face in accepting them as partners in one world community.

Acknowledgements

All of these essays have appeared in other places, although they have been edited for inclusion here. Chapter I, "A Gospel Mandate," first appeared under the title "Letting Go: A Sociotheology of Relinquishment," *Presbyterian Women.* Chapter II, "The Prophetic Tradition," was the presidential address to the Association for the Sociology of Religion, published under the title "How Prophecy Lives," in *Sociological Analysis* 33, no. 3 (Fall 1972), and it also appeared as a chapter in *A Sociotheology of Letting Go* (1977). Chapter III, "Toward a New Civil Religion," was one of four lectures sponsored by St. Joseph's University (Philadelphia) Theology Department in a series entitled "Living Humanly and Living Well: Some Ethical Challenges" and presented on April 11, 1985. Parts were adapted from "The Future of First Amendment Provisions Regarding Church-State Relations," in *The Future of Our Liberties,* ed. S. C. Halpern (Greenwood Press, 1982). Chapter IV, "The Future of Altruism," was given as the Paul Hanley Furfey Lecture, sponsored by the Association for the Sociology of Religion at St. Michael's College, Toronto, August 21, 1981, and was published as "Commitment to Altruism" in *Sociological Analysis* 43 (1982): 1–22. Chapter V, "Altruism as Public Virtue," was given as the Sorenson Lecture at Yale Divinity School, November 8, 1983. Chapter VI, "Social Justice and the Right To Use Power," was the presidential address to the Society for the Scientific Study of Religion, Knoxville, Tenn., 1983, and was published in *The Journal for the Scientific Study of Religion,* 23 (1984), pp. 329–339. Chapter VII, "Education for Justice," was presented at a national assembly, "Global Crossroads: Educating Americans for Responsible Choices," Washington, D.C., May 18, 1984, and was published as "Altruism and Social Justice," in the *International Schools Journal* (Autumn 1984), pp. 13–22. Chapter VIII, "The *Magnificat* and the Economy," was prepared for a United Church of Christ project and was later published in *Sisters Today* 56 (November 1984). Chapter IX, "A Socio-Theology of Relinquishment," was presented as part of a conference entitled "What Is Liberation Theology?" sponsored by Georgetown University Department of Theology, on June 10, 1985. Because of the occasion for which each of these essays was written, there is a necessary repetition of some basic themes. They bear repetition in order to be tested in different contexts. All previously published essays are reprinted here by permission of the publishers.

Thanks are extended also to the *New York Times* for permission to quote from articles which appeared in that newspaper, © 1972, 1981 and 1985 by the New York Times Company.

Some elements of the publishing of a book are new and others are deeply rooted in the past. As with the book of which this is a sequel, Ron Marstin's fine editing moved it to publication. For this, I am deeply grateful. Sister Grace Pizzimenti and Sister Esther MacCarthy once again did that critical reading prior to first presentations which, done with honest candor, provides the sober critique and humorous chiding that finally give form to dreams and clarity to ideas. I wish to express special thanks to Sister Raymond Loretta Kelley, who graciously did a final reading of the manuscript. There are new people to thank, people who have been the inspiration for the new essays. They are the sisters and the brothers who respond to the calls, demands, invitations, pleadings, challenges, petitions for new methods of teaching, critical social analysis, programs of transformative action, renewal of Constitutions, direct action for housing, food co-ops, public hearings, social-justice oriented retreats, biblical studies, social action, lifetime commitments, and other essential elements of an effective movement toward a truly just world of vibrantly living peoples. Old and young alike, they are there and they are continually going forth and returning, telling those stories that bring new hope. To them, together with the struggling organizing poor, this book is dedicated in faith, hope and love. They provide the inspiration and the evidence that a transformed world is in the making. Their faith points to the fact that God is with the poor as they reach out to claim their rights as human beings. Some of them are: Barbara Mellan, Dolores Harrell, Sue Murphy and Gertrude Barron, Jeanne Gallo and Marie Noel, Sylvan Smith and Geraldine Butler, Joyce McMullen and Margaret Lanen, Linda Bessom, Helen Wright and Mary Congo. They are not legion. They are chosen by God. There are others, many others, who cannot be named lest they die, and some are men.

I

A Gospel Mandate

The world's poor are reaching out to take what is rightfully theirs. How to respond to that fact is a major challenge facing Christians in the late twentieth century.

In its efforts to provide for a population of 4.8 billion, the world political economy has in fact settled for a rough triage—one third is well provided for, another third fairly well, and the remaining third is quietly allowed to die. It does not have to be this way.

Despite dire predictions that population growth would outstrip our capacity to produce goods and services and overwhelm the available space, a United Nations projection sees world population tapering off by the year 2110 at around 10.5 billion. Given the fact that current population amounts to an average of only 98 people per square kilometer of arable land,[1] 10.5 billion is a population we can provide for quite well if we have the imagination and the will to do so (Murphy, 1984).

Some initiatives sponsored by the Vatican and by the World Council of Churches have been criticized as too socialistic, but it should be clear to Christians that any solution to the global poverty problem is unacceptable as long as it gives up on a third of the world's people. The churches have already sanctioned the efforts by poor peoples to organize for the realization of their human rights. The task now is to help the rest of us respond appropriately to the new demands being made on us.

For those who are not poor—those of us at the high end of the life-expectancy, the low end of the infant-mortality scales—

the spectacle of poor people organizing and demanding the goods they need to survive is likely at first to frighten us, to cause us to cling tighter to what we have. Dealing with that fear, that resistance, is a special task for Church people.

When the rich young man in the Gospel asked what more he needed to do to win eternal life, Jesus said, "Go, sell what you have and give to the poor . . . and come, follow me." And when the young man went away sad because he had so many possessions, Jesus remarked, "How hard it is for a rich man to get into heaven—harder than for a camel to get through the eye of a needle" (Mk 10:17–27).

Earlier, after John the Baptist accused his hearers of sin, they sought repentance and asked him what they needed to do. He said, "If you have two coats, give to them who have none; and, if you have food, do the same" (Lk 3:3–10).

The Gospel demands of those who are not poor that they release their hold on the things the poor need for survival. In Gospel terms, blocking some from access to available food and clothing is sin; repentance means making the food and clothing available to those who need it.

It is a mandate we are likely to find a bit hard to take. When we have struggled to provide for ourselves and our families, it is not easy to think of sharing what we have with others. We feel put upon by the Gospel's stark directive. It is a feeling Jesus apparently understood: his yoke is easy, he reminded us, and his burden light (Mt 11:29).

Computer technology has created an unemployment problem that some seem to think can be resolved only by a "lifeboat" ethic—with survivors floating on a sea in which many must be lost. But while it is true that computers can now do many of the tasks that breadwinners were once paid to do, a new perspective might suggest a new solution to the problem.

One such perspective is that of women, who have been for centuries primarily responsible for the care of those needing food, clothing and shelter. If we accept all the world's people as our progeny, caring for them as we would our families, some solutions to the problems of producing and distributing goods and services become unacceptable.

Arms production, with its potential for killing the family, is no solution to the unemployment problem. Moreover, since we need as much food as possible to care for the human family, higher profits are no excuse for curtailing production. And as long as human needs require durable goods, it makes no sense to make things that wear out quickly. We need to find alternate ways of providing goods and services, and it is only fear that prevents our seeking them.

It is that fear that kills those who seek a different way—the fear that, in 1980, killed Archbishop Oscar Romero and four women missionaries, Jeanne Donovan, Maura Clark, Ita Ford, and Dorothy Kazel, in El Salvador. It is the same fear that kills the poor.

We can do better. We can alter the definition of who is included in the human family. We can redistribute responsibilities for governance, work and family care. We need not be afraid. We are not alone.

II

The Prophetic Tradition

In recent years the prophetic voice in the Judaeo-Christian tradition has merged increasingly with the voices of the old and the new left. The Popes have followed the old left in calling for a redistribution of wealth and the new left in calling for the redistribution of power.

Eighty years of Catholic attempts to respond to the social revolutions of the nineteenth and twentieth centuries reached a climax in Pope Paul VI's *Call to Action*, written in 1971, the eightieth anniversary of Leo XIII's *Rerum Novarum*. The letter marked a long struggle within the churches of the first world, a struggle taken up in the late nineteenth century, to affirm the legitimacy of basic changes in social structure—including the gamut of political, economic, class, and cultural organization.

Pope Paul noted the breakdown of national boundaries and the emergence of multinational corporations "which are largely independent of national political powers and therefore not subject to control from the point of view of the common good." Multinational organizations, he pointed out, "can lead to a new and abusive form of economic domination on the social, cultural and even political level" (Paul VI, 1971a, #44).

People today legitimately aspire to "a greater sharing in responsibility and decision-making," Pope Paul noted, recalling the point made by Pope John XXIII (in *Mater et Magistra*) that "admittance to responsibility is a basic demand of man's nature, a concrete exercise of his freedom, and a path to his development" (ibid., #47).

"It is to all Christians that we address a fresh and insistent call to action," Pope Paul wrote. And he continued:

> It belongs to the laity, without waiting passively for orders and directives, to take the initiative freely and to infuse a Christian spirit into the mentality, customs, laws and structures of the communities in which they live. . . . It is not enough to recall principles, state intentions, point to crying injustices, and utter prophetic denunciations: these words will lack real weight unless they are accompanied for each individual by a livelier awareness of personal responsibility and by effective action" (ibid., #48).[1]

It was a prophetic stance that the Second Vatican Council clarified. As a result, local churches and individuals could freely take an initiative and still feel they were speaking in the spirit of the council, even if they were not affirmed by Church administrators.

The Medellín conference of Latin American bishops, bent on implementing the decrees of Vatican II, adopted in 1968 a policy directive of prophetic dimensions. It was derived from the pedagogical methods used in Brazil, Chile and elsewhere in Latin America, methods aimed at rapid basic education of peasants not only in literacy but also in social, economic, and political awareness. This educational process, which came to be called "conscientization," refers to "learning to perceive social, political, and economic contradictions and to take action against the oppressive elements of reality" (Freire, 1970, p. 19). The method was originally named and made popular through the action-reflection program of Paulo Freire, the brilliant scholar and teacher exiled from Brazil, and of his sponsor and friend Dom Helder Camara, then the archbishop of Recife in northeast Brazil. Both were held in disrepute by their government, which later coopted the program in its own interests.

In introducing their new stand, the Latin American bishops said:

We are at the beginning of a new historic epoch in our continent. It is filled with the hope of total emancipation—liberation from all servitude—personal maturity and collective integration. We foresee the painful gestation of a new civilization (Medellín I, 1970, p. 9).

Bishop Eduardo F. Pironio, General Secretary of the Latin American Episcopal Council (CELAM), explained further:

Medellín hurts because it demands radical changes and an abandoning of certain privileged positions. The Medellín commitment demands courage. Renovation also demands meditation and the sincere search for new roads. It would be dangerous to change for the sake of change, without understanding the significance and the demands of change (ibid.).

In 1970, the Canadian Conference of Bishops, in conjunction with the Canadian Council of Churches, prepared for implementation a program derived from the Medellín documents and affirming a change of focus "from the alleviation of the results of poverty to an elimination of its causes" (Canadian Bishops, p. 8). Specifying that programs of social concern will be focused on eliminating the causes rather than on alleviating the results of poverty implies two goals: (1) to deinstitutionalize political, social, and economic structures that oppress the third world, and (2) to construct, in the process of "conscientization," those social forms that are developed by people reflecting and acting on their own oppressive situation (Medellín I, pp. 65, 76, 81).

How prophecy lives in our times can be seen in the way attitudes have changed since Karl Marx's charismatic condemnation of entrenched economic interests. First there were denials of Marx by the establishment, then attacks on other prophetic voices, the rise of false prophets, and co-optations of prophecy. There followed a struggle to free prophecy from established power and self-interest and to replace, with the prophetic message, understandings imprinted on people's consciousness by a long process of socialization. Finally, awareness grew of the meaning of the statement that "religion is the opium of the people." Established churches are now examining oppressive social structures and ordering policy changes, despite concerted resistance by the agents of transnational wealth. As that happens, it becomes the task of sociologists of religion to test seriously claims that the relationship between Christianity and socialism is far different from what established interests say it is (*Latin America Calls*, pp. 4–5).

Like other prophets, Marx seriously denounced structured evil and placed much of the blame on religious institutions. Existing structures spring from the social relations that grow up around production, he noted, and are maintained by control of consciousness through the family, education, recreation and religion. In the elite's control over violence through the military and over the unknown through the mass media, he saw the tools of oppression.

Does the biblical tradition provide any warrant for discerning the prophetic voice in today's transition to socialism (Sweezy and Bettleheim)? According to the *Jerome Biblical Commentary*, the prophet in biblical tradition stands in judgment on the nation. The prophet's task is to call his co-religionists to repent because their public and private lives belie the biblical message they claim to be living.

The Old Testament prophets were distinctly of Israel when they spoke "the fearless revelation of the moral will of Yahweh, the God of Israel's covenant" (*Jerome Biblical Commentary*, p. 227). The prophet is called "one made to speak" (ibid., p. 225). A false prophet was not so much one who intended lies as one who was so caught up in his own culture that he came to see Yahweh as willing what was in accord with Israel's preference, rather than as reprimanding Israel when she acted contrary to Yahweh's will (ibid., p. 226). Prophets sat in judgment on the institutions of Israel and became the conscience of the nation (p. 227). This judgment on the nation constituted a new role in the religions of the Near East, and it has become part of the tradition of Western culture since that time (p. 229).

In insisting on the social implications of the religion of Yahweh, the prophets were not proposing anything new but were recalling a known, although much ignored, morality (p. 233). Vawter notes:

> Poverty was never sentimentalized by the prophets of the Old Testament; it was regarded as an undesirable thing. The poor man was not just because he was poor, but the existential fact could not be ignored that poverty and injustice were frequent companions. It was the evil of other men that had created this situation and the whole prophetic effort was directed against this evil (ibid.).

The New Testament prophetic voices are those of John the Baptist and Christ himself (Mt 11:7–15), and they reiterate the demand to repent and to "bear fruit that befits repentance," disclaiming any hope of salvation merely because one is a son of Abraham. John calls his brethren a "brood of vipers" and warned them of the wrath to come unless they repented. But when they begged to know "What then shall I do?" he answered, "He who has two coats, let him share with him who has none; and he who has food, let him do likewise" (Lk 3:8–11). Christ continued this theme by promising the kingdom to the poor (Mt 5:3). Current prophetic voices get their leverage from this Gospel root and scholarly Church research of the most recent years rejects any claim that the promise of the kingdom to the poor in spirit includes the rich who are "spiritually detached" from their wealth. The *Jerome Biblical Commentary*, in treating both prophecy and the beatitudes, denies that the kingdom is promised by Christ to anyone but the materially poor (I, p. 233, and II, p. 70).

Who stands today in the Judaeo-Christian tradition of prophecy? To answer the question we have to find those who cry out against injustice and who seriously chide established economic and political interests, those who are rich, and those whose task it is to enforce the law, despite its demonstrated oppressive quality. Further, we must look for those who, in carrying out the mission of biblical justice, are inveighed against, defamed, allowed no public forum by the prevailing powers and who, though found to be credible by the oppressed themselves,

are publicly subjected to suspicion as subversive and privately
viewed by those who are financially secure or relatively safe in
the system as demented, naive, foolish, dangerous, and evil.

What such prophets say must be in line with the Gospel,
even if their personal lives are reported as at least maverick in
quality and even immoral from the point of view of those embed-
ded in the system. With this Gospel criterion, one can include as
prophetic witnesses Philip and Daniel Berrigan, the Catonsville
Nine, the Milwaukee Fourteen, and other witnesses to peace.
Among these are Mahatma Gandhi, Martin Luther King and
Dom Helder Camara—the former two familiar with imprison-
ment and victims of death by violence—defined as prophets of
action. Prophets, too, are Frantz Fanon and Paulo Freire, both
products of third world culture and first world professional train-
ing, both exiled for their teaching but internationally recognized
as humane and Christian. So, too, are Cosmas Desmond, O.S.F.,
Ernest Cole, Govan Mbeke, and Chief Albert J. Luthuli, all of
South Africa and all known for the human compassion of their
denunciations. They have suffered exile, house arrest and cur-
tailment of their careers by their government for revealing its
structured evil. Cesar Chávez, Angela Davis and George Jackson, by the witness of their lives and their writings, have also
been recognized as holy by the oppressed and as evil by the system.

But if we include as prophets these and the many others
who speak for the oppressed poor, then we have to include Karl
Marx, whose cry of condemnation regarding religion was so pen-
etrating, and the reaction of established systems so violent, that
the meaning of what he said was obscured for a hundred years.
Only in our times is it safe to name him as prophet and only because his message is indistinguishable in some respects from that
of the priest.

Listen to these priestly words:

Capitalism has often bred too much misery, too much
injustice, too much bitterness and strife. Industrializa-
tion itself has not brought these abuses. The wretched

system that came along with it has brought evil into
being (Paul VI, 1968, #26).

Again:

The earth's goods must be divided fairly and this right
of every man to a just share comes first. Even the right
to private property and the right to free enterprise must
yield to justice. All other rights must help, not block,
this basic right of every man (#22).

Yet again:

From time to time the good of all demands that private
property should be taken over by the state. This should
be done if landed estates have grown too great or cause
dire poverty; or if they hamper seriously the prosperity
of the whole community (#24).

And finally: "Left to itself, the workings of international trade
tend to make the rich richer, while the poor develop slowly if at
all" (ibid., #8).

Since 1970 I have read these passages to large groups of
Catholics in various U.S. states, South Africa, and Zimbabwe
(when it was still Rhodesia). In no case did more than ten people,
from audiences ranging from fifty to over a thousand, recognize
these as Gospel words. Each group senses the similarity of these
ideas to principles they associate only with dialectical materialism and assumes they must be rejected by followers of the Gospel. Yet they are direct quotations from Pope Paul VI's 1968
encyclical *Populorum Progressio.*

To have a copy of that document was considered subversive
in northeast Brazil in 1968. From the point of view of systems
analysis, prophets are deviants. That is because they question
processes already institutionalized in the system, the manner in
which decision-makers are planning, programming, implementing, administering, and communicating their policies and val-

ues, and the effect of these on the people. They criticize what established organizations are doing to their members as persons and appeal to the masses to dissociate their affections from them. Most of all, they make people more aware of their own collaboration and involvement with established interests. They point out to the masses, whose cooperation with the system is essential for its functioning, how its program is evil in the light of the values they preach and how they, too, are evil to the degree that they help prolong its injustices. The prophet's definition of sin is the heart of the prophetic message.

Prophets differ in their insights, and what they have to say differs according to the conditions of the times. But, whatever the social change they call for, the very fact that they are calling for change makes them a threat to the establishment. That is why, from the leaders' point of view, prophets must be silenced—unless the leaders choose to repent. "Beware of men. They will hand you over to the Sanhedrin and scourge you in the synagogues. You will be dragged before governors and kings for my sake, to bear witness before them and the pagans" (Mt 10:17–19). When Jesus said that, he was saying what any knowledgeable sociologist would say, because he had already taught his followers to reject the existing distribution of wealth and privilege. He knew that those in power must either destroy the prophets, once they have stirred up the people, or accept their message. Jesus was killed because he stirred up the people—the reason all prophets must either be heard or die.

When the prophets are not killed or relegated to the category of despised fool, they are usually coopted by the system, their message emptied of its system-rejecting qualities or given only token response. Given status within the established order, they become quiescent or at least sufficiently reinterpreted to preclude the need for immediate structural changes. But if injustice is real, efforts to protect the system will not prevent further disenchantment on the part of the people—a growing apathy and malaise which can lead to work stoppages, sickness, death, or spontaneous uprisings. All of these responses are part of the process of withdrawing affection from the norms of the system, and they can be expected when the message of the prophet fits the experience of the masses. Repression of the message brings only temporary reprieve while the very repression prepares for revolt.

From the point of view of those who have control over the established system—labor, industry, trade, the unknown, and the uses of violence—the message of the prophets is potentially destructive. To the degree that priests celebrate the system—performing the rites that bless established interests and focus the psychic energy of the people on their appointed tasks—they and the prophets will be opponents. Those in power, fighting for their own interests and believing they have a right to do so, will provide the means for the destruction of the prophet. What is more, with the support and blessing of the priests, they will be convinced that, in doing so, justice and truth are on their side.

Only a reformer, as distinct from a prophet, can be tolerated by the system and, even then, only the reformer whose reforms will least deflect energy from established goals. To be patient with reformers, to protect them, and even to affirm them when there is dissatisfaction in the ranks are among the operating functions of the system. Channels of education, recreation, religious celebration, and mass communication carry the intellectual criticism needed to control the reformers and their message.

Because reformers accept that the system is fundamentally capable of serving the people, they will point to injustices, inefficiencies and neglects that need attention but will not call for basic restructuring. Reformers are often hired to assure people that the system is organized in their interests and that the leaders are listening and caring for them. The system provides funds, personnel and services to reformers—military and police assistance at times—because their "healthy" criticism boosts the spirits of the moderately disenchanted, permitting them to hope that things will be better. For new role players, too—like immigrants and young people, who are likely to look the system over critically before buying into it—reformers can smooth the passage to acceptance and commitment.

The prophet's message, on the other hand, calls for basic structural change. The message is that world poverty is so endemic it cannot be resolved by traditional forms of service: there needs to be a redistribution of both power and wealth. It is a message that is more likely to get a hearing among the two-thirds of the world's population with too little power or wealth to feel confident about their survival. For them, the prophet's message is credible. They will risk trying it out. They have everything to gain and little to lose.

The struggle between prophecy and the forces ranged against it is especially likely to be waged in the areas of family life, education, and religion. Consciously or not, education systems reinforce established views and religions confirm them as holy (Dawson). In calling for social structures in which newly-aware people relate to one another as peers, not as sons or daughters, prophets are striking at the roots of traditional societies of the West and East. Because educational systems are still barely experimenting with this style of relationship and because religious systems still confuse family and community models, no first or second world society has yet yielded to the prophetic message.

Established churches perform two different social functions: (1) reinforcing commitment when self-interest, unrest, loneliness, dissatisfaction, disappointment, anger, and other distractions pull people away from the common effort of staying alive and developing their potentials; (2) providing an environment for dissociating affections from the system in time of needed social change. It is because the church gathering focuses on human destiny and purpose—on our common destiny rather than individual advantage or disadvantage—that established society needs a celebrating church in its midst to restore the energies of the members and proclaim the legitimacy of its ways. (It is this function of religion that Durkheim analyzes in *Elementary Forms of the Religious Life*.) By its ritual of celebrating life and expressing love and hope, by threatening punishment for those who sin, and by linking sin with violations of existing law and order, the church reinforces the social purposes of the group, confirming the goodness of the status quo. It can affirm in an unreflecting way the goodness of conformity to law and order. Prayers for national leaders or for the success of national, state or local projects and encouragement to participate in the national endeavor provide the establishment with an affirmation that is affectively reinforced whenever the worshiping community meets. The very regularity and ritual quality of the worship service guarantee that its affirmation is relatively unreflective and that what gets affirmed is the established structure.

But when a church continues this function during periods when established authorities are responsible for manifest injustice on a large scale, it plays a major role in reinforcing the evil. The injustice may affect members of a single society or, in the case of war or trade or other agreements among powerful nations, it may affect powerless peoples the world over. If the worshiping community regularly prays for the leaders of church and state but its ritual expresses no concern for migrant workers, students, black inner-city dwellers, Appalachian miners, prison inmates, or victims of disasters, war and exploitation, not only are the exploited given no reason to rejoice but church members who remember the original Gospel and are aware of current forms of oppression will find their participation less meaningful.

In many cases, churchgoers, not wanting to admit that the church has been coopted, simply stop coming, stop caring. Those who remain—predominantly those who want the system to continue—so lack the vital drive for renewal that the church becomes a relic, contradicting its essential role of celebrating God's will, which is interpreted as being the good of humanity (Küng).

The process of disenchantment readies the community to hear a prophet, to listen to anyone who can show the meaning of what is happening and propose alternatives. If the disenchantment is advanced, members of society experience anomie and alienation and become polarized—between those who sense that the old order must be saved at all cost and those who sense that it must be destroyed. The most reactionary and the most radical have in common a willingness to use force, in destroying the enemy. Moderates, unwilling to use force, draw together in an effort to deal with the explosive situation.

In polarized settings, many proposals are advanced, often with unclear or unexpressed assumptions about what must be

saved. Sometimes proposals for change or resistance are implemented before their implications are understood, so eager are
people to do something to relieve their anxiety about impending
doom. Only when the program has been implemented do they
see what they have collaborated in and, depending on how they
assess the situation, either direct their energies in the same or
other directions or withdraw from action, feeling incapable of
coping with or being responsible for what happens.

Given the function of mass education, it is hardly surprising
that little education is geared toward understanding social process. The result is that people who are not accustomed to participate in decisions of their community—and that means most
people in elite-structured societies—look to religious systems for
a means of escape, not so much from oppression itself as from
the anxiety generated by the discovery of oppression.

That discovery has a way of disrupting family and other
small community gatherings. When injustices are revealed, people take sides. Prophets arise, offering various resolutions—salvation outside the system, or through personal transformation—
resolutions that require no change in structures whose functioning is increasing the oppression of powerless populations. A gospel is preached that bears no relationship to the structure of
systems, a gospel that can be realized even within oppressive
systems, a promise that the Lord will destroy evil leaders on account of their personal sinfulness.

Against that background, one channel of modern prophecy
has chosen to focus on eliminating the causes of poverty rather
than on alleviating the results. Marx was the preeminent representative of this tradition in the nineteenth century. As established interests translated his message, it came to mean that he
advocated the overthrow of capitalism by violent revolution and
the rejection of religion because it was the opium of the people.
The result was that those with secure power were long lulled into
ignoring the problem he addressed—the increasing oppression
of people caused by the established division of labor.

The following story ran in the *New York Times* on July 27,
1972:

Brazil's Roman Catholic bishops in the last two months have begun to stake out a clear position as defenders of the little man and champions of human rights in a country where varying degrees of repression are the rule.

Since early in June four regional groupings of bishops in Brazil, the most populous Roman Catholic country in the world, in effect accuse Brazil's military-led government of ignoring the interests of Indians and the poor rural squatters in the national rush for economic development. They have also publicly accused military and police authorities of arbitrary arrest and torture.

Such statements by Brazilian Catholic prelates are not entirely new, but the unequivocal wording and unanimity of the recent pronouncements are new here. The bishops individually and collectively have also been careful to make it clear that their positions are based on church social doctrine, not on political doctrine.

Dom Antonio Fragoso, bishop of Crateus in northeast Brazil, a diocese of 350,000 peasants and one of the poorest in the country, was in the United States to make a plea for political prisoners and to talk with Daniel Berrigan and Cesar Chávez. He was refused permission to preach to Portuguese-speaking Americans in the diocese of Fall River, Massachusetts and his presence was ignored in the archdiocese of Boston, even though a request for a meeting had been placed well in advance.

A week earlier, while Fragoso spoke to representatives of government and private agencies about the imperialism of American foreign trade policies in Brazil, the foreign minister of Brazil was negotiating with the President of the United States for more of the aid that allows Brazil to have the most rapidly increasing GNP in the world although ninety percent of its people live at subsistence or below.

In that country, prophets who had provided a method of development so successful that whole communities became literate within periods of six weeks to six months were either in exile or under interdict as subversive, dangerously communist, and despicable. One is Paulo Freire, author of *Pedagogy of the Oppressed*, a method of conscientization among peasants, who was exiled from Brazil in 1964 and later worked with the World Council of Churches in Geneva. Another is Dom Helder Camara, now-retired bishop of Recife in northeast Brazil, who is the author of *Spiral of Violence* and other books revealing the oppressive quality of Brazilian society and who was treated with contempt in the Brazilian press. Then there is Fragoso, whose diocese was subjected to systematic repression because he "stirs up the people" to seek their rights under the law. Belgian theologian José Comblin, author of *A Theology of Peace* and *A Theology of the City*, was rector of the regional seminary in Recife until he helped design a program aimed at preparing seminarians for the struggle for justice. His permanent visa was withdrawn on March 24, 1972, when he returned to Brazil after a short vacation. Accompanied to Lisbon by a Brazilian policeman, he was simply told that, besides having used "Marxist terms," he had associated with Dom Fragoso.

These are Comblin's reflections on a meeting held in Crateus in November 1971:

> Naturally the meeting was affected by what had recently happened in the diocese and by the threat of its recurring. . . . The diocese's present situation can be explained by the prophetic position taken collectively, or by various movements, or by the bishops, in the name of the diocese. In relation to other Brazilian dioceses, Crateus seems to be alone in its position of prophetic tip. That position and that isolation made the recent repression inevitable.
>
> There is no reason to think that the repression will lessen. There are no new factors that will make it lessen since the Church has taken upon itself to defend, represent, and conscientize the people. Such functions are not carried out by public authority. Their program is based, rather, on law and order and silencing the people. Thus, any prophetic action will be vigorously repressed, especially if such action is aimed at the masses (Comblin, p. 2).

Bishop Fragoso described a meeting at which the Brazilian government invited Brazilian theologians to discuss their concept of church. He related that, after the meeting, the Brazilian police drew up for themselves their own description of the church in Brazil. For them, the conservative church, which cooperates with the government, is supportive of their position and is to be encouraged. It includes only a few dioceses. The reforming church, which includes most of the dioceses, calls for some basic changes in Brazilian society. Although these calls are troublesome and to be resisted, the church on the whole can be tolerated since it accepts society as it is. Then there is the progressive church. This church, including only thirty dioceses, is subversive and to be repressed. It is here that Fragoso's diocese of Crateus is assigned. In these dioceses the police already had tortured priests and lay people who participated in programs of conscientization. Surveillance, invasion of privacy, and interruptions of meetings were the order of the day. The progressive church, defined by the state as dangerous and, therefore, condemned by it for destruction, is recognized by theologians in Brazil as more directly in line with the directives of Vatican II and the Medellín conference than are the other two sectors of the church.[2]

That the prophet is the enemy of the state can be seen dramatically in the comparison of sentences given to William Calley and Phillip Berrigan. Calley was responsible, together with his higher officers, for killing villagers, defenseless citizens, in an undeclared and unjust war. Once found out, he was tried to save military face. Because what he did was intended by the program with which he was associated, he received only a symbolic sentence. Phillip Berrigan performed a symbolic act against the records of men at war to fulfill the prophetic function of raising to consciousness the evil of war. He received an excessive punishment (six years) because, from the point of view of the system, his act was far more destructive of the morale of American society than was Calley's.

But Berrigan helped generate the malaise that will make it psychically impossible in time for the youth of the country and the world to continue to celebrate the system. If the prophets are heard, young people will be unable to internalize its norms or believe enough in its values to draw energy for the tasks needed to stay alive. From the point of view of system maintenance in its present style, the prophet is more dangerous than the killer. Yet from the point of view of maintaining the human race, the prophet is necessary for its survival. Prophets take the cause of humanity as their own, and risk life, reputation, and career. The risk involves their own destruction. Prophecy lives by the death of the prophets and the life of their word (Camara and Fanon), by their symbolic gesture (Berrigan and Gandhi), or by their action toward social change (King and Freire).

III

Toward a New Civil Religion

It is an ethical assumption of our culture that, as long as there are not enough resources to go around, we have a right to take care of ourselves and our own—no matter that choices based on self-interest run counter to the religious doctrine of altruistic love. Judging social behavior in a framework of altruism is written off as utopian, as too idealistic for practical realization. Even those who profess a belief that Jesus, in dying for our sins, gave us an example of selfless service in the interest of the poor define as heroic any attempt to emulate him. His example is a model for saints, not ordinary people.

Suggestions for structural reforms toward altruistic ends elicit gentle or firm correction from colleagues; scholarly work grounded on the assumption that altruistic behavior is now normal is treated as an embarrassment (Sorokin, 1958; cf. Chapter IV). But the assumption that self-interest determines human behavior needs to be examined. On the basis of the time-honored tradition of self-interest, we have justified war as a means of killing enemies, competition for scarce resources as a way of running an economic system, national interest as a tool for keeping the lid on third world struggles for self-development, and triage as a solution to the problem of over-population. These policies assume that we live in a world where the resources needed for life are scarce and there are too many people. But suppose that has changed. Suppose there are now enough goods, provided they are produced and used responsibly, and that population is limited not by forced control but by human choice. Would the claims of self-interest then be morally persuasive? What would happen to the argument that self-interest is a characteristic of human nature and that grace builds on nature so defined? Given adequate resources, that thesis is no longer functional for rallying people to social action; it no longer makes sense.

Even though a declining population no longer needs as much land as it once did to sustain a decent life, Social Darwinism has emerged in its modern form of sociobiology as ideology for preserving territorial domination: religion is subsumed in a theory that explains human relations as a *quid pro quo* exchange among interested neighbors, each genetically determined to preserve his or her own progeny.[1] Religious fundamentalism, assuming that human nature is so sinful that the world is beyond redemption, offers salvation only in quitting this world for heaven or Armageddon, which is only hastened as the world tumbles toward nuclear holocaust. That sounds like ideological support for the arms race (Solomon). Were there no real question that world resources are too scarce and world population too prolific, there might be less reason to examine ideologies—like the "lifeboat" ethic—that justify our secret wish to destroy defenseless people lest they destroy us. But the evidence needs to be weighed.

Since 1980, global population projections have predicted a leveling at about 10.5 billion around the year 2110 (Murphy, 1984, pp. 2–3). Since 1983, careful studies by the Population Reference Bureau of world food production, mineral resources, and energy potential suggest that we can provide for that number of people under certain conditions (Murphy, 1983, 1984; Bouvier, 1984). In 1984, Lester Brown, of Worldwatch, came to a similar conclusion. The necessary conditions include responsible stewardship of resources, curbing upper- and middle-class greed, building for use not profit, investing in clean air, eliminating nuclear arms production, and the immediate sharing of emergency resources with nations experiencing natural or man-made disasters.

The social action that would achieve these conditions, because it is action more calculated to benefit others than oneself, would require the kind of motivation and incentive that comes from shared beliefs and values—especially religious beliefs and values—that tend to get swallowed up, during times of scarcity, by pragmatic concerns for self-preservation. But in times of sufficiency, we are faced with a different choice: either to contrive scarcity in order to justify our keeping more than we need or could even use, or to free our religious impulses to follow the path mapped in the Scriptures.

Christianity is founded on an ethic of sharing unto death. It provides absolutely no rationale for preferring genetic progeny to the stranger or even to the enemy. It calls for altruism as the normal group ideal (Mt 5:43–48). While it affirms the quality of neighborliness and the value of sharing resources within the community, it extends the notion of community beyond tribal limits to the whole human race.

Today the feasibility of sharing resources with the human community rather than hoarding them for ourselves is a problem with a technical solution. That is, the limitations on global sharing are now no longer either biological or technological—they are social, economic, political and, ultimately, religious. They challenge our idols and confront our biases. They demand review of our myths. They challenge our civil religion. They unmask us.

There is more than enough food in the world to feed the world's people. Despite this fact, a half billion people, one-tenth of the world's population, will die of malnutrition, and 1.1 billion are living in absolute poverty, with their infant mortality rate high and their life expectancy low. Our present response is in the tradition of triage.[2] It includes the following plans, all of which leave the poor to die: to reduce the production of food that cannot be sold on the world market by paying farmers not to produce it;[3] to continue a policy of planned obsolescence so that those who have access to wealth can discard what they have, purchase more, and keep the economy "healthy"; to continue to exclude struggling third world nations from trade and aid planning groups because of their lack of power and wealth, and thus to continue the production of goods they cannot use and telecommunication systems to which they have little or no access (Cerni, 1984); to control the development of independent third world nations on the basis of the harmony or disharmony of their ideologies with the perceived national self-interest of dominating nations; to educate the next generation of children of the non-poor to belief that such action is moral and blessed by God, thereby risking the possibility that these children try to resolve contradictions they experience by escape into drugs, alcohol and suicide in an anomic society.

This description may sound crass, even brutal. It is. What could possibly humanize this unnecessarily inhumane process? Nothing, if survival of the fittest is the law of the land; otherwise, a new civil religion. But a civil religion is limited to one nation-state, and what can one country do in the face of a global struggle for survival? Maybe that very limitation of religious focus on one nation is the problem with the practice of civil religion now. There is nothing in the notion of religion that limits teaching about salvation to refer to that of only a single nation. There is much in the history of religion, however, that does so limit its teaching. At the turn of the century, Emile Durkheim, one of the founders of modern sociology, concluded from his astute examination of religion in practice among primitive peoples and in the Europe of his day that the god most people worship is the nation that nurtures them. Karl Marx, examining religion in the middle of the nineteenth century, concluded that its concern was limited not to nations but to classes within nations. To Marx, religion was the opium of the people because it taught the dispossessed to endure now in order to be assured of heaven hereafter and also that the dominant class should rejoice in the blessing God bestows upon them in reward for their enterprise, thus reinforcing in worship the inequities of the status quo. Edward O. Wilson, sociobiologist, sees religion today performing its rightful function when it celebrates the interests of its adherents and supports both their aggression against enemies and the male-dominated structure of their bureaucracies (Wilson, 1978a). All of these observers are interpreting what they see. However, is what they see the worship of a just and loving God or is it idolatry (Richard)?

World poverty challenges us today in a new way. It presents itself not so much as an overwhelming problem tearing at our hearts and eliciting expressions of anguish in the face of an unsolvable problem, but rather as the challenge of a complex problem with a technical solution, solvable if we choose to address it. It tears at our conscience, not at our hearts. We know today that the problem is social, political and economic—that is, calling for a change in norms—and is not biological or technological, beyond physical or moral possibility. Because of media coverage, we know it as real. A half billion people who lack sufficient food to stay alive and 1.1 billion without sufficient food, clothing and shelter are not easy to forget. Because of the greater accuracy of computer calculation, we know that 57 percent of the people live in countries with GNPs so low—below $750 per capita—that they are characterized by high infant mortality (over 86 per 1,000 live births) and low life expectancy (below 55 years of age on average). We know, too, that this problem does not lie in scarcity of food and other resources for living but rather in lack of money to exchange for available resources (United Nations, 1980, p. 45).

But who has this money that others need for life and what are they doing with it? The non-poor have it and they are spending it to acquire more food, clothing and shelter than they need and, in some cases, than they can use (Murphy, 1984, p. 6). Laws protecting property and assumptions about the market as well as access to power provide the means; religions provide the justification.

We can check these facts from our own experience if we are among the non-poor. What we find will challenge our theories of a free-market economy bringing the greatest good to the greatest number, and will threaten our assumptions—couched in terms of Jeremy Bentham or of Divine Providence—of the hidden hand (of God) guiding the free enterprise system (Kopkind). We will hear ourselves indicating in our rhetoric grave concern that centrally-planned economies are invariably atheistic and totalitarian and, hence, justifiably threatened with obliteration by nuclear weapons. Yet it appears, from the point of view of those countries experiencing poverty, that the operation of the world economy in its capitalist forms is similarly devoid of the presence of God and no less high-handed in decision-making about access to goods and services and who designs them.

What shall we do, then, we who are interested in the dynamic potential of religion for moving the world toward effective solutions of problems of human survival and enhanced quality of life for all peoples? Is there a religious dimension to this very human problem? Does God figure in the political economy? According to national surveys done by the Gallup poll over the past several years, most Americans believe in God (94 percent) and about 70 percent of them believe God acts in history. But what are they taught about how God acts in history? There is substantial evidence that people are taught to have faith in the economy as somehow blessed by God in its present form (Novak, 1984). Few are taught to look at starvation in Ethiopia and to question the structure of the American economy as a primary cause and one that they personally should seek to change. Few ever hear a challenge to our political economy as a necessary response to problems of world poverty and human development. Few opinion leaders even raise such questions, and those who do so risk being categorized as wrong, naive, or subversive (Gallup, 1984). Examination of the curricula of our seminaries, theology departments, religious education programs and pastoral ministry programs indicates we are just beginning to introduce a justice and peace agenda as constitutive elements of a preaching of the Gospel. And yet pastorals on racism, peace, and the economy, following the mandate of Vatican II to shape a religious response to social injustice, strike a responsive chord in the hearts of the American people. Why is this so?

Sociologists, looking at the practice of religion in American society in the mid-1960s, thought they observed a religious factor that gave the people the capacity to stand together in judgment on the nation when manifest injustice within the system called for change in structures or behavior. Robert Bellah called that force civil religion. Civil religion is a relatively new concept, a term given new meaning in the 1960's and itself a contribution to the national culture.[4] The insight it highlights is this: we have little need to fear church establishment at the present time; what we need to fear more is the loss of a focus for shaping an altruistic public conscience, a conscience that can generate and preserve public concern for the survival of the poor when their labor is no longer needed in an automated and computerized production system.

Civil religion in America refers to a national faith that has a creed and moves the people of the nation to stand in judgment on the laws of their own state when they perceive that those laws violate what the creed affirms. It also moves people to rejoice in their nation-state when they experience it as realizing the values of the creed. Bellah extracted the term "civil religion" from Rousseau's *Social Contract,* where it was used with a narrower meaning to refer only to a set of beliefs that support the political authority of the state. In Rousseau's analysis, these included belief in the existence of God, in a life to come, and in the reward of virtue and the punishment of vice, with an added dictum regarding the "exclusion of religious intolerance." Rousseau, as social philosopher, was recommending a way to civic harmony through support for civic authority, a development of the ancient *pietas.*[5]

Bellah added new meaning to the term. He shaped it to signify something more specifically religious in the sense of transcending the law of the land, recognizing a higher authority, and capable of passing judgment on the law. He introduced the term in 1967 as a concept for sociological analysis of a phenomenon he thought could be distinguished from several others. At that time he wrote:

> While some have argued that Christianity is the national faith and others that church and synagogue celebrate only the generalized religion of "the American Way of Life," few have realized that there actually exists, alongside of and rather clearly differentiated from the churches, an elaborate and well-institutionalized civil religion in America.[6]

The main tenets of this faith, which he extracts from the Declaration of Independence and the Constitution, are the beliefs that God created all people equal and endowed them with certain inalienable rights.

"Civil religion at its best," Bellah explained, "is a genuine apprehension of universal and transcendent religious reality as seen in or, one could almost say, as revealed through the experience of the American people."[7] The critical quality of this religion, he claims, is that people who believe in it can call upon it as a framework from which to judge the nation when it violates the rights of people or fails to protect them in time of unrest. "It is of the essence of the American civil religion," he writes, "that it challenges institutional authority."[8]

In Bellah's analysis, civil religion is a normative reality. Essentially prophetic, it stands in contrast and opposition to the folkways of the people; it judges the idolatrous tendencies of particular forms of Christianity and Judaism. In civil religion he locates the prophetic function of calling the nation, including its civil leaders, to account whenever they fail to protect the rights of any members as people "created equal."

When Bellah wrote again about civil religion in 1974, he was bemoaning the failure of the civil rights movement and the antiwar movement to mobilize the nation to act effectively against racism and war. It is no longer possible, he wrote, for Americans to hide from the fact that the covenant implied in the civil religion that dates from the birth of the republic is now broken.[9]

Political theorists and activists who have taken a position on separation of church and state are disturbed by Bellah's passion and, for this reason, question his objectivity as a sociologist. The intent of his analysis, they claim, is to bring about a condition of critical self-examination from the perspective of religious symbol and fervor while they, who favor a secular ethical perspective, believe that the failures of states are better addressed with the aid of cool reason and secular values.

When Bellah's writings turned more prophetic than analytic, his social science colleagues chided him for lack of objectivity. However, students of religion espoused his cause. As the debate continues, it pursues two main questions: whether the covenant is in fact broken, since racism still characterizes America, and whether the focus of civil religion has moved from the nation to the world society.[10]

In modern theological speculation, the intellectual and religious interest in the idea of civil religion is directly associated with a new political consciousness. The attention of theologians has been drawn to the growing problems of a world economy that outstrips the power of the state and the corresponding need for some type of association capable of addressing in a serious way the ethical and social problems generated by new international centers of power.[11] The survival of the poor requires a public religion with an informed conscience. This need is hardly served by the churches' simply affirming their diversity or by social commentators' allocating religion to the private sphere, two themes commonly heard in the last decade among researchers on the relation of church and society (Berger).

But something more dynamic seems to be alive in the churches' reflection on ministry today, something not bounded by the nation-state but addressing the political economy in world pespective and judging it exploitative and unjust in its support of small wars, resistance to developing nations, and control of access to needed resources (Steidl-Meier). An ethic of justice and peace is a moving force in the churches, speaking through missions throughout the world and coming back to the dominant nations in stories of struggling "basic communities," of missionaries risking life and dying along with villagers who often scarcely know why forces of international power invade their villages, fund their enemies and destroy their lives (Cussianovich).

Growing among theologians who are globally-oriented and motivated by concerns of social justice is a recognition of human rights that transcend nationality and call for reclamation of the land, the chance to work, the opportunity to share in production, to be educated, to become fully human. These new demands find affirmation in organized religion. It would appear that among Catholics, Protestants and Jews there is a new shared religious commitment and the moral strength that this implies. It includes a high valuing of genuine participatory democracy with special concern for the poor as equals. This moral force is calling to account the laws of the land and insisting on due process whenever the poor, the ill, and the old are excluded from decisions affecting the uses of the common wealth. There is a growing sense among the religiously-committed that full participation of formerly oppressed peoples in the decisions that affect their lives is no idle dream but rather the wave of the future. Moreover, the focus of their religious concern, deeply biblical in form and content, is not simply the nation-state but world society. It has a force that challenges theologies oriented toward entrenched interests and church policies that idolize the nation.[12]

From this point of view, privatized religion—the wave of the twentieth century and a comfort to those bent on resisting liberation movements—is recognized as the ideology of a secularized state comprised of atomized human units.[13] Concern for the survival of peoples other than one's own interest group seems to be rooted in a "genuine apprehension of universal and transcendent religious reality" standing in judgment on those laws of the nations that permit the destruction of other peoples defined as outsiders and enemies. What characterizes this religion is altruism. It is part of a new religious consciousness within churches.

The new awareness owes nothing to the narcissism of much current religious feeling. Rather, it celebrates the so-called folly of the Judaeo-Christian doctrine of the love of one's neighbor, the giving up of one's life for the stranger.[14] Though it is the central value of all world religions, altruism—the disinterested love of the other—is once again the object of a radical, politically-motivated, scientific challenge (Neal, 1982).

A recent academic rationale for the selective development of peoples is provided by sociobiology, a synthesis of biology, ethnology, sociology, and psychology. It claims as its central thesis that altruism, like all behavior, is basically motivated by a determination programmed in the genes to preserve the tribe. It is a programming to which even the richest religious and humanitarian efforts are necessarily subservient.[15] According to the theory of Wilson, what he calls "hard-core" altruism—giving one's life that others may continue to live—extends only to one's family, tribe and, in a mild way, to one's nation. The motive of self-sacrifice is always the extension of one's own gene pool. All other kindness to others—what he calls "soft-core" altruism—is extended only on a *quid pro quo* basis. Under this rubric, one gives in proportion to an expected return, where the expected return is the advancement of one's own kin's interest, even at the expense of that of all others. Religion, he says, is intentionally a part of this soft-core altruism.[16]

Sociobiology is a new form of Social Darwinism. It provides no rationale beyond self-interest for our helping the poorest nation to survive; if it is not in our interest to help we can ignore with good rational conscience the plight of another people. At the same time, it rationalizes aggression against strangers even if they are struggling third world nations or peoples within our own society (cf., for example, the institutionalization of apartheid in South Africa or the treatment of Haitian immigrants in the United States). It rationalizes conflict between poor nations. Religious love of neighbor is redefined as selective of one's kin. The otherness of God is denied; God becomes our survival interest. In sum, sociobiology aggressively denies the possibility of a religiously-derived ethic of love that springs from grace and faith, is inclusive of a world population and challenges the reality of a genetic drive for the survival of some at the expense of others.

Just as there begins to be a wider recognition of the human rights of peoples to survive and to have access to life-supportive resources—as evidenced by the United Nations covenants and by recent church documents[18]—there arises this "scientific" argument against the very possibility of real altruism. The clear implication of this argument for public policy is that to plan solutions for the problems of need on the basis of a utopian dream of universal love would be not only impractical but threatening to the survival of the species.[19]

The new valuation of human rights, on the other hand, suggests a growing world consensus that peoples have a right to live and that we can no longer will the death of others by defining them as enemies and so as legitimate targets in war or as hopelessly poor and so beyond human capacity to rescue. This new human-rights ethic suggests a radical breakdown of the divine right to privilege and the human right to hoard under the rubric of radical private property. It prompts the hypothesis that our current assumption of self-interest is calculated to preserve white ascendancy in an increasingly non-white world. The current advance in our understanding of human rights, historically already moved beyond slavery and serfdom, now moves beyond caste and class. We can no longer presume the right to use the labor of others simply because we can pay for it. Human beings are no longer mere factors in the economic equation for production of goods and services. We work for life and all have a right to it.

People no longer divide on this issue along the lines of denomination or ethnic identification. The critical division is now within each church and ethnic group, cutting across older alignments and making allies of strangers. The concrete issues include: opposition to war, to arms production, to indiscriminate use of nuclear energy and to the disposal of nuclear waste near unprotected populations; mistreatment of political prisoners; the affirmation of minority-group rights to employment, good education, health care, and choice of residence area; the human right to migrate across national boundaries. The fundamental issue, across many religious persuasions, is whether one's religious commitment includes a social calling, beyond a willingness to help alleviate the results of poverty, to participate in the elimination of its causes.

All three religious traditions in the United States have biblical roots that call for the treatment of human suffering and all have historically been involved in delivering health, educational, and welfare services. But the three also share a tradition of social justice, one which now goes well beyond the requirements of a legal justice—honoring rights of property acquired by fair exchange of the stipulated collateral—and calls for the elimination of poverty. The growing church consensus on human rights accounts for the fact that Pope John XXIII's *Pacem in Terris*—with its thesis that peace, poverty and human rights are the central concerns of the committed Christian—is a universally acclaimed document.

How human rights are to be defined is the subject of two United Nations covenants on human rights, together now called the Bill of Rights (United Nations, 1978). They won the thirty-five votes needed to become official United Nations policy in 1976. The United States was not among the affirming voters. Not until October, 1977 did the covenants receive the signature of the U.S. President, and they do not yet enjoy the necessary treaty ratification of the U.S. Senate. The U.S. State Department is still trying to "correct" what it calls the "collectivist emphasis" in the United Nations' affirmation of the right of peoples to self-determination (*GIST*, February 1985).

Many of the rights described in the covenant entitled "Civil and Political Rights" are familiar to us, but that entitled "Economic, Social and Cultural Rights" contains many we still consider privileges rather than rights, such as the rights to free medical care, access to free education through college, care in retirement regardless of amount of work done, access to the benefits of employment, full employment, the right to form labor unions, and the rights of nations to self-determination and to the free use and enjoyment of their natural wealth and resources.[20] To the poorer nations, the latter category of rights is of principal concern at present. For some twenty million of our own fellow citizens also, these rights are not available in our economic program, itself the mainstay of our political system (cf. report on hunger in America, *New York Times*, February 27, 1985, p. 1).

The excitement of the moment is that our traditional religious systems are affirming these rights.[21] In so doing, they are reactivating a membership alienated in recent decades by the churches' conventional insensitivities to human oppression and their substitution of concern for so-called "spiritual" poverty for concern for the actual poverty of people struggling to stay alive. True, such insensitivities still characterize some affluent, mainline, local churches in America. Here members are often more interested in issues of personal tax-exemption than in sharing the common wealth with the unemployed, for whom the national economy can provide no jobs. But when the churches and synagogues do hear a religious call to action for justice, they bring to public consciousness critical questions of domestic and foreign policy—questions about the denial of human rights to health, education, and welfare services in this the world's most affluent nation; questions about the dispossession of the unemployed and underemployed; questions about our support of apartheid in South Africa; questions about covert aid to the *contras* in Nicaragua, and about the need of an informed press to provide an accurate understanding of what is happening in South Africa, the Middle East, Northern Ireland, Central America, the Philippines and Cambodia; questions about who has the power to shape public conscience and to what purpose; questions about the structure of world capitalism; about the implementation of the United Nations' human rights covenants; questions about the survival of peoples.[22]

As the churches raise public issues as matters of religious concern, issues in which we as a nation play a predominant role, they experience new pressures from the state. The pursuit by the FBI of religiously-motivated protesters against the Vietnam War is a case in point. So, too, is the threat of denying to the churches their tax-exempt status on the argument that they are moving outside the area of legitimate religious discourse. Today, the sanctuary movement, rejection of aid to the *contras* in Nicaragua, and resistance to the use of tax monies for arms production align the churches against the state and reflect an informed public conscience. There seems to be a new life to civil religion standing in judgment on the nation.

In the past, the churches themselves have sometimes—for example, in distinguishing "faith and order" concerns from "life and work" concerns—separated the spiritual agenda from the social. Even today, some inside and outside the churches criticize theologies that incorporate the social agenda, calling them merely political ideologies in religious guise. But, increasingly, the churches are defining the economic, political, and social concerns characterized by injustice and violence as religious concerns. Such religious convocations as the Second Vatican Council, the international conferences of the World Council of Churches at Uppsala, Nairobi and Vancouver, and the Detroit "Call to Action" Conference of 1976 called their members to active participation in bringing about social justice as a religious responsibility. The bishops' pastorals on racism in 1979, on peace in 1982, and on the economy in 1984 and 1985 are products of these earlier convocations of church people. Moreover, while the themes of liberation theology are political, economic, and social, they are also eminently religious and rooted in Scripture.[23]

As the churches pick up this social justice agenda as their common cause, the emphasis is frequently missed by the media, which concentrate instead on narcissistic themes in the religious and other areas of popular culture.[24] The new focus of the churches is not narcissistic but public. The relegation of religion to the private sphere should itself be recognized as a political strategy. Growing out of a specific ideology of containment and facilitating the development of a specific type of secular society, it attempts to render ineffective the social justice component of the Judaeo-Christian tradition by defining only privatized religious behavior as specifically religious and suggesting that social and political dimensions of worship are secular rather than religious. Berger's sociology of religion is a case in point, as is Novak's advocacy of the economy (Berger, 1974; Novak, 1984). The social justice tradition is more concerned with shaping the future than it is with sustaining the past. It calls for a review in the public forum of what are defined as properly religious concerns. Here in the making is a new civil religion whose agenda is global and whose object is the salvation of all peoples. It is moving into public consciousness. Altruism is its central element, self-interest its counterpoint in struggle.

♦ IV

The Future of Altruism

What is it about the world today that accounts for the recent introduction of the concept of altruism into the research, theorizing and teaching of sociology and social psychology? One report concludes that "we know more about hate, aggression, and prejudice than about love, sympathy, and cooperation" (Wispe, 1978). But we should not jump to the conclusion that that explains current interest in the subject. A better explanation might be found in the United Nations covenants on human rights, which touch on areas that have traditionally been the focus of altruistic concern—the provision of health, education and social security to people deprived of these services (United Nations, 1976). The nations of the world are struggling for effective implementation of these covenants, and it is worth asking whether that struggle may not be the cause of the new scholarly interest in altruism. If the disciplines of sociology and social psychology are addressing world conditions, we need to ask: To what end and with what effect? And what does the current interest in altruism have to do with the study of religion?

From 8000 B.C. to 1850 A.D., the world's population grew to a billion. A century later, world population numbered two and a half billion. Twenty-five years later, in 1975, it had grown to four billion. Contrary to earlier projections, the most recent UN estimate is that world population will level off at ten and a half billion by 2110.[1]

The population is very unevenly distributed over the world's land space, and people have very unequal access to the food, energy and materials needed to provide shelter, security and human development (Sivard, 1980). Eighteen percent of the people live in countries with a developed technology and market economy. These are the twenty-four richest nations, and their per capita GNP stood at $U.S. 7,046 in 1980. Nine other developed countries, characterized by a centrally-planned economy and containing nine percent of the world's people, have an average per capita GNP of $3,091.[2] The remaining, developing countries have seventy percent of the world's population and a per capita GNP of $890 (Population Reference Bureau, 1980).

It is much harder to stay alive in the developing countries than in either of the two developed groups. Life expectancy, 72 years in developed countries, is 57 years in developing countries. The infant mortality rate, 20 per 1,000 live births in developed countries, is 110 in developing countries. The rate of natural increase—that is, the ratio of birth rate to death rate—is .6 in the developed world, 2 in developing countries. That means that, at present rates, the population in the developed world will not double for 111 years; in the developing countries, it will double in 34 years. Some developed countries have already reached zero population growth; all of them are expected to reach that point by the year 2000. Further, while the more developed nations have 59 persons per square kilometer of arable land, the less developed have 128.[3]

A physical quality-of-life index (PQLI), fashioned from infant mortality, life expectancy and literacy figures and scaled to run from zero to 100, provides a non-income measure of human well-being. For the world, the PQLI stands at 65. For developed countries it is 92, with only four countries falling below 90. For the developing countries, it is 55, with several countries dipping into the twenties and teens.[4]

All first and second world countries, with the exception of Albania and Mongolia, have an annual per capita grain consumption of over 600 pounds. For most of the other countries it is between 200 and 400 pounds, although for 32 of the developing countries it is less than 200 pounds. Yet, according to the UN research staff, the world is not short of food. Rather, "if all the food that is produced in the world could be equitably distributed, there would be more than enough for everyone." Even though 400 million are undernourished today and double that number suffer from malnutrition of one kind or another, the problem lies in the imbalances of the world economy, which leave large numbers of people—most of them in Africa, Asia, and Latin America—without the money to pay for food which is plentiful (United Nations, 1980, p. 45).

The problem lies in world trade and aid programs, in production plans in first and second world countries, in the control of the land and resources in developing countries by the developed countries. It is a political and economic problem. It is also a problem whose solution requires a measure of altruism on the part of those who control the world's resources.

The United Nations Bill of Rights, which became official U.N. policy in 1976 after twenty years of commission work and ten years of signature-seeking, indicates a growing world awareness of the right of people to the resources of the land in which they live.[5] The bill formally recognizes and incorporates in treaty arrangements all the rights associated with the basic right of people to live, including the rights to food, health care, education, social security, and work.

Although the white populations of the world are declining and will make up less than 20 percent of world population by 2000, they inhabit—in North America, Australia, and New Zealand especially—some of the most sparsely populated land in the world. People per square kilometer of arable land average 98 worldwide. The figure is 3 in Australia, 53 in the U.S., 381 in India, 954 in Bangladesh. Yet the immigration policies of sparsely populated countries are unrelated to other peoples' need for more space. On the contrary, immigration policies in the U.S., Australia and New Zealand allow migration from first world populations that do not need more space while limiting migration from other and especially non-white groups.

Our rationale for this policy is the "lifeboat" ethic, which has been formalized in academic analysis by Garrett Hardin (1974) and offered in 1979 as a policy guideline to shape public opinion. In 1974, Hardin asked his colleagues to assume that approximately two-thirds of the world is desperately poor, and only one-third is comparatively rich. Metaphorically, each rich nation amounts to a lifeboat full of comparatively rich people. The poor of the world are in other, much more crowded lifeboats. Continuously, so to speak, the poor fall out of their lifeboats and swim for a while in the water outside, hoping to be admitted to a rich lifeboat, or in some other way to benefit from the "goodies" on board. What should the passengers on a rich lifeboat do? This is the central problem of "ethics of a lifeboat" (*Bioscience* [October 1974], p. 561).

He takes no account of long-range population trends recognized since 1965. He ignores the injustice in the developed world's control of the developing world through transnational corporations and assistance programs like those of the Organization for Economic Cooperation and Development (United Nations, 1980). Some scientists would agree with Hardin's suggestion that hardhearted realism is a better guide to interpretation of evidence than is softhearted altruism. Others disagree.[6]

Roger Ravelle, then director of the Population Center at Harvard University, argued in the early 1970's that the carrying capacity of the earth is 35 billion people. From both World Bank and United Nations population projections, it is clear we will never reach that number. The reason we fail to provide for the present population, the U.N. researchers make clear, derives from a problem not of capacity but of access:

> The root of the hunger problem is distribution. In many countries where malnutrition is prevalent, up to half of the cultivated acreage is growing crops for export to those who can afford them rather than foodstuffs for those who need them. Thirty-six out of forty of the poorest and hungriest countries in the world export food to North America (*New York Times*, July 16, 1981, p. A4).

Human need is graphically displayed in statistical tables, in television stories, in data presented by committed researchers through such channels as the United Nations information services. Is there something in the makeup of developed nations that makes them insensitive to the need? In first world nations—North America, Western Europe, Australia, New Zealand, and Japan—is there anything about their democratic capitalism that legitimates selfishness? Do second world countries, with their centrally-planned economies, do any better for peoples in developing nations?

These questions need to be pressed in light of some current trends in public policy. The build-up of arms, for example, has reached such proportions that we are capable of destroying every city in the world several times over.[7] These weapons are available for use wherever third world peoples, in their struggle for survival, become embroiled in small wars—for example, in the Middle East, Southern Africa, Northern Ireland, Southeast Asia and, especially, Central America. The use of nuclear energy for weapons as for peacetime projects is also well under way in many parts of the world, with third world areas being selected for dumping the radioactive waste. In the absence of safe means for its disposal, this waste endangers life for the present and successive generations.

Third world peoples are predominantly non-white. Within their countries of origin as in the countries to which they migrate, they are being forced into apartheid-like residential patterns on the basis of policies dictated by self-interest. Cases in point include El Salvador, Guatemala, Nicaragua, Chile, Brazil, South Africa, Mozambique, Tanzania, Angola, Northern Ireland, Palestine/Israel, Cambodia, Vietnam, Korea, Afghanistan, East Timor, the Philippines, and any area within a country from which a group of people is being removed, at the expense of its basic survival needs, in order that another group can expand an already affluent life.

The premise that legitimates these organizational arrangements is shaped by academic disciplines like political science and economics. It is a premise of self-interest. The question of altruism is this: How can people control the inclination to act in their own interest in order to enhance the interests of others who are not of their group? Auguste Comte, who coined the word, used altruism to refer to "unselfish regard for the welfare of others" (Wispe, 1978, p. 304). Until recently the word has not been used by other sociologists, with the exception of Pitirim Sorokin, the first sociologist to devote volumes to its consideration (Sorokin, 1950). Sociology as a discipline did not concern itself with altruism until the mid-1970's, when Wilson introduced it as the central variable of sociobiology. For psychologists, who began their investigation of the concept in 1965 (Campbell), the question of altruism is basically the question of individual commitment to group survival. Why and under what conditions will one person give up life for the sake of another or for the sake of the group?

For some, altruism is seen as a genetically-transmitted disposition. Others interpret it as a product of social indoctrination. Others hold it is a distinguishing constituent of human, as distinct from animal, nature. For yet others, it is a gift of the gods (D.T. Campbell in Wispe, 1978, p. 41). In the late 1940's sociologist Sorokin and psychiatrist Frantz Fanon both chose altruism as their central variable, both assuming it to be a quality of our common humanity. At the end of a long career devoted to the study of social and cultural dynamics, Sorokin chose to spend his retirement in the study of altruistic love and behavior (1950a). A lifetime spent researching the causes of the chaotic conditions of Western society led him to the task of the reconstruction of humanity (Sorokin, 1948). Materialistic culture, he held, is superficial and lacking in any absolute values to direct the conduct and thinking of its members: "At the present time there is no value or norm, whether relating to God or to the institutions of marriage or private property, that is equally accepted by all and regarded as universally binding on all" (ibid., p. 48). The heart of modern decay is moral, he concluded (ibid., p. 184; see also Sorokin, 1950b). In his search for an overarching ethical norm, a synthesis encompassing truth, beauty, and goodness, Sorokin focused on love-energy to effect needed social transformations. "We know next-to-nothing about the properties of love-energy," he wrote. "They have hardly ever been investigated from this or any other standpoint" (Sorokin, 1950a, p. 42).

Fanon, a black psychiatrist from Martinique, worked with Arabs in North Africa who had become emotionally disturbed in their struggle against French colonial exploitation. In explaining the guilt of those who, faced with the challenge of rescuing a needy stranger, failed to do so, he cites Karl Jaspers:

> There exists among men, because they are men, a solidarity through which each shares responsibility for every injustice and every wrong committed in the world, and especially for crimes that are committed in his presence or of which he cannot be ignorant. . . . Somewhere in the heart of human relations an absolute command imposes itself: In case of criminal attack or of living conditions that threaten physical being, accept life only for all together, otherwise not at all (*La culpabilité allemande*, in Fanon, 1967, p. 89).

Unlike Jaspers, Fanon did not believe in God as the origin of the "absolute command," but he was convinced of the naturalness of altruism as a human trait, and his life, as described in the same book, reflected that conviction.

Lauren Wispe's *Altruism, Sympathy, and Helping* (1978) is at present the most comprehensive report on the extensive social psychological research that has been done. She reports on studies of when and under what conditions an individual will reach out to help somebody in need or distress, and studies of why, when people do not help others, they blame the victims for their lot. This type of research seems to have been stimulated by a dramatic instance of failure to help—the Kitty Genovese case in 1964—that now appears in almost every introductory social psychology textbook (Albrecht, 1980, pp. 283–84).

Most psychological research limits itself to the conditions under which a person is more likely or less likely to help another. The following are some of the findings: people are more likely to help if they are alone than if they are in a group; in a small city rather than in a large urban center; if the recipient has a manifest need; if it is not a great inconvenience; if it creates joy for the giver; if children are socialized to it early in life (Wispe, 1978; Rushton, 1980). Some researchers claim not only that altruism exists but that it is essential to human life; others, that it is essentially self-gratification. Dr. Robert B. Cialdini, professor of psychology at Arizona State University, is ready to abolish as non-existent the concept of "behavior carried out to benefit another without anticipation of rewards from external sources," while J.P. Rushton (1980, p. viii) begins his study by stating, "Altruism is essential for the existence of society." He wants to find out "why people live with pro-social consideration for others by being honest, generous, helpful, and compassionate and desist from engaging in such anti-social behavior as lying, cheating, stealing, and aggression." DeVore and Morris (1977) point out that so much of our behavior is calculating, selfish, and deceitful that we erect elaborate religious, social and linguistic networks to mask underlying motivations, motivations springing from genetic drives to enhance our chances of establishing our inclusive fitness for survival. But then Rushton (1980, p. 10) presents a volume of evidence to demonstrate that altruism is learned and can be improved by social learning.

While altruism, as a clearly-defined variable for social psychological research, does not appear in the literature prior to 1965,[8] its forerunners are reviewed exhaustively by Gordon Allport in the first edition of the *Handbook of Social Psychology* (1954) under the concept of "sympathy." Here are reviewed works ranging from Plato to Ashley Montagu, in which sympathy is used to explain human affiliative behavior. But only in the work of Max Scheler does Allport (1958, p. 27) note an analysis sufficiently refined to distinguish altruism—dedication to the service of others as a humanitarian or religious commitment—from a variety of helping behaviors. The reported research does not indicate a specific focus on altruism. The early research explores the theme of cooperation as distinct from competition (M. Mead, 1937; M.A. May and Doob, 1937). The more recent research of the 1950's is done under the rubric of group dynamics, industrial relations, and psychotherapy (Schacter, 1959). Today, standard introductory texts in social psychology contain one or more chapters on egoism and altruism (Albrecht, 1980). Here, both sociobiology and learning theory seek to explain altruistic behavior as genetically rooted in selfishness or learned in the socially-trained self-interest of exchange. The mysterious philosophical root of altruism noted by Jaspers or the transcendent root described by Sorokin does not appear in psychological research.

Without a doubt, the specific work that brought sociologists to dwell directly on the concept of altruism in the past few years was Wilson's *Sociobiology: A New Synthesis*, published in 1975 by Harvard University Press. The subject moved quickly into focus in Van der Berghe's revision of *Man and Society: A Biosocial View* (1978) and emerged in several introductory textbooks and annuals with a speed that suggests it is being pushed hard. With *Sociobiology* and subsequent volumes—*On Human Nature* (1978a) and *Genes, Mind and Culture* (1981)—Wilson extended his study of insects, for which he had won recognition, to the study of humans. He claimed to be introducing a new scientific discipline that subsumes social organization and all human culture under human biology. The energy for the making of culture, he said, comes from a genetically-rooted drive to perpetuate the genetic pool that the individual shares with kin.

What makes Wilson's thesis of particular interest to sociologists of religion is his identification of altruism as a core concept for analysis:

> Scientists are not accustomed to declaring any phenomenon off-limits, and it is precisely through the deeper analysis of altruism that the new discipline of sociobiology seems best prepared at this time to make a novel contribution (1978c, p. 23).

He begins with several examples of altruistic behavior on the part of insects that suggest parallels with human behavior. He explains that he does this not to claim that humans and insects are characterized similarly by mind, but to show that the impulse to altruistic behavior "need not be ruled divine or otherwise transcendental, so we are justified in seeking a more conventional biological explanation" (ibid., p. 24). His "more conventional" explanation gives altruism a genetic origin rather than the cultural or religious roots that have been used to explain it historically.

Wilson agrees that the "form and intensity of altruistic acts are to a large extent determined by culture" and that "human social evolution is obviously more cultural than genetic," but his critical claim is that "the underlying emotion, powerfully manifested in virtually all human societies, is what is considered to evolve through genes" (ibid.). From the start, he focuses on the self-interest in altruistic behavior, claiming:

> No sustained form of human altruism is explicitly and totally self-annihilating. Lives of the most towering heroism are paid out in the expectation of great reward, not the least of which is a belief in personal immortality (ibid.).

In trying to demonstrate the "ultimately self-serving quality of most forms of human altruism," Wilson distinguishes two basic forms of cooperative behavior. Of one, he says:

> The bestower expresses no desire for equal return and performs no unconscious actions leading to the same end. I have called this form of behavior "hard-core" altruism, a set of responses relatively unaffected by social reward or punishment after childhood.
>
> Where such behavior exists, it is likely to have evolved through kin selection operating on entire, competing family or tribal units. . . . We expect hard-core altruism to serve the altruist's closest relatives and to decline steeply in frequency and intensity as the relationship becomes more distant.

For soft-core altruism, the other form of cooperative behavior, he also posits an evolutionary selection and a cultural shaping: "The capacity for soft-core altruism can be expected to have evolved primarily by selection of individuals and to be deeply influenced by the vagaries of cultural evolution." But it is strikingly different in motive and form from hard-core altruism: "Its psychological vehicles are lying, pretense, and deceit—including self-deceit, because the actor is most convincing who believes that his performance is real." It is this uniquely human form of altruism that he claims subsumes all of culture, including religion. And soft-core altruism—rather than the hard-core variety, which is limited to relatives who share genes—is the object of sociological analysis.

There can be no mistake about his claim:

> Pure, hard-core altruism based on kin selection is the enemy of civilization. If human beings are to a large extent guided by programmed learning rules and canalized emotional development to favor their own relatives and tribe, only a limited amount of global harmony is possible (ibid. p. 25).

It is Wilson's intent to show how, through the *quid pro quo* exchange of the soft-core type, relationships among strangers can be sustained. In describing soft-core altruism, he says:

> Reciprocation among distantly related or unrelated individuals is the key to human society. The perfection of the social contract has broken the ancient vertebrate constraints imposed by rigid kin selection. Through convention of reciprocation, combined with a flexible, endlessly productive language and genius for verbal classification, human beings fashion long-remembered agreements upon which cultures and civilizations can be built (ibid.).

His pursuit is consistent. He raises the question himself: "To what biological end are the contracts made, and just how stubborn is nepotism?" In the struggle for power, "international cooperation will approach an upper limit, from which it will be knocked down by the perturbations of war and economic struggle, cancelling each upward surge based on pure reason." Then "the *imperatives of blood and territory* will be the passions to which reason is slave" (ibid., emphasis added).

Lest some be abashed at this claim, Wilson assures his audience: "One can imagine genius continuing to serve biological ends even after it has disclosed and fully explained evolutionary roots of unreason." His optimism rests in his belief that "human beings appear to be sufficiently selfish and calculating to be capable of indefinitely great harmony and social homeostasis." It is in this selfishness that he roots the social contract: "True selfishness, if obedient to the other constraints of mammalian biology, is the key to a more nearly perfect social contract."

Genes are always self- or family-serving, Wilson concludes, while culture is always self-serving:

> Human altruism appears to be substantially hard-core when directed at closest relatives, although still to a much lesser degree than in the case of the social insects and the colonial invertebrates. The remainder of our altruism is *essentially soft* (ibid., emphasis added).

Religion and morality he locates in this soft-core type of altruism which, as noted above, is shaped by deceit, including self-deceit. Of morality, he says that the rules we devise are those that will canalize our territoriality and xenophobia. Thus, our rules of fair play and safeguards to private property are developed to favor contracts of advantage to our tribe and determine who will receive our favors at a given point in history. He notes that "human beings are consistent in their codes of honor and endlessly fickle with reference to whom the codes apply," because this important distinction is "between the ingroup and the outgroup but the precise location of the dividing line is shifted back and forth with ease" (ibid., p. 27).

Obviously, this description fits the foreign and domestic policies of governments with power over others. What Wilson does is to claim a genetic base for such policies, thus rendering self-interest scientifically legitimate and incapable of reform by any transcendent religious or moral conversion. Prompted by Kohlberg's theory of moral development—which identifies stages in the adequacy of moral decision-making, ranging from judgments dictated by fear of punishment to those based on universal principles of justice—Wilson asks, "Can cultural evolution of higher ethical values gain a direction and momentum of its own and completely replace genetic evolution?" His answer:

I think not. The genes hold culture on a leash. The leash is very long, but inevitably values will be constrained in accordance with their effects on the human gene pool. The brain is a product of evolution. Human behavior— like the deepest capacities for emotional response which impel and guide it—is the circuitous technique by which human genetic material has been and will be kept intact. Morality has no other demonstrable ultimate function (ibid, p. 28).

Wilson leaves his audience, the readers of the Harvard alumni magazine, to ponder what reviewers have called "a brilliant and insightful analysis of human social behavior," although the author had earlier acknowledged that year (1978) that sociobiology "is still rudimentary science. Its relevance to human social systems is still largely unexplored" (1978b, p. 14). We should ponder whence comes its reputation for brilliance.

It is Wilson's hope that a morality grounded in scientific materialism, rather than "traditional" religion, will better achieve a true humanization. "Sainthood is not so much the hypertrophy of human altruism as its ossification," he writes, adding, "The true humanization of altruism, in the sense of adding wisdom and insight to the social contract, can come only through the deeper scientific examination of morality" (1978c, p. 27). That means incorporating morality into an effective mutual exchange between interested partners.

Religion is considered in the context of myth. As one cultural element of soft-core altruism, it is useful for shoring up energy for cultural exchange; it also has a place as a binding force of group solidarity. But there is no place for traditional religion's notion of God as creator and redeemer, for which a learned substitute will have to be found for effective human development. Wilson writes:

The sociobiological explanation of faith in God leads to the crux of the role of mythology in modern life. It is obvious that human beings are still largely ruled by myth. Furthermore, much of the contemporary intellec-

tual and political strife is due to the conflict between
three great mythologies: Marxism, traditional religion
and scientific materialism (1978a, p. 193).

Marxism is the secular equivalent of traditional religion, according to this theory. On the other hand, Wilson thinks it will prove
itself wrong in history, while theology will retreat to the creation
myth from which it cannot be driven easily. But he warns:

> Make no mistake about the power of scientific materi-
> alism. It presents the human mind with an alternative
> mythology that until now has always, point for point,
> in zones of conflict, defeated traditional religion (ibid.,
> p. 195).

He then outlines how this final assault on religion will pro-
ceed, according to his preferred myth of scientific materialism.
In his theory,

> every part of existence is considered to be obedient to
> physical laws, requiring no external control. The sci-
> entist's devotion to parsimony in explanation excludes
> the divine spirit and other extraneous agents. Most im-
> portantly, we have come to the crucial stage in the his-
> tory of biology when religion itself is subject to the
> explanation of the natural sciences. As I have tried to
> show, sociobiology can account for the very origin of
> mythology by the principle of natural selection acting
> on the genetically evolving material structure of the hu-
> man brain.

He adds:

> If this interpretation is correct, the final decisive edge
> enjoyed by scientific naturalism will come from its ca-
> pacity to explain traditional religion, its chief competi-
> tor, as a wholly material phenomenon. Theology is not
> likely to survive as an independent intellectual disci-

pline. But religion itself will endure for a long time as a
vital force in society (ibid.).

In this analysis, then, he has done with religion what he did with
morality, and earlier with logic and reason, the very tools of the
scientific discipline. That is, he has subsumed them under the
evolutionary force of natural selection in genetic self-interest.

But he is not yet finished. Interested as he is in the policies
that derive from his theory, yet knowing that the theory is not
yet established as a mode of investigation of human behavior, he
poses this question: "Does a way exist to divert the power of religion into the services of the great new enterprise that lays bare
the source of its power? (ibid., p. 193). "The great new enterprise" is a moral consensus historically lost in the split between
religion and Marxism (p. 195). This division can be healed, Wilson thinks, by adopting the scientific ethos in their place. In com-
menting on the "second dilemma" involved in choosing among
the ethical premises inherent in man's biological nature (p. 4) or
"among our innate mental propensities" (pp. 195–96), he states:

> If religion, including dogmatic secular ideologies, can
> be systematically analyzed and explained as a product
> of the brain's evolution, its power as an external source
> of morality will be gone forever and the solution of the
> second dilemma will have become a practical necessity
> (p. 201).

Thus, we can root our political and economic choices in an essential selfishness and limit the choice of alternatives to our own
self-interest. Given the exclusion of other races evidenced in the
statistics presented earlier in this chapter, Wilson's conclusion—
a first world position—hardly promises life for third world peoples.

Few social theorists would agree, given current evidence,
that human behavior can be logically reduced to biological in-
heritance. Wilson himself recognizes that sociobiological theory
does not imply by itself that human social behavior is determined
by genes. It allows for any one of three possibilities: (1) the hu-

man brain has by now so evolved that it is freed from genetic control; (2) human social behavior is still under genetic constraint but, since all genetic variability has been exhausted, we are all under the same constraint and hence have the same potential; or (3) since the human species still exhibits some genetic variability among individuals, further biological capacity for social behavior may evolve. Wilson considers the third alternative to be correct (1978b, p. 1).

Anthropologists, sociologists, and psychologists, who define altruism as a basic human trait or one that can be learned, differ from Wilson in their premises for the investigation of cultural differences. They adopt the first or second thesis. Ashley Montagu is one. He writes:

> What sociobiologists do not fully understand is that, as a consequence of the unique history of human evolution, humankind has moved into a completely new zone of adaptation, namely, culture, the human-made part of the environment; that is, through the learned part of the environment humans respond to the challenges of their environments, and not through the determination of decision action of genes (Montagu, 1980, pp. 8–9).

From this perspective, educability becomes the major focus of human development and the constraints of genetic selfishness are no longer the limiting frame of political action.

There is an enormous difference in the implications of these two positions for the setting of public policy—policies regarding the protection of territory by armed resistance against the "invasion" of strangers, that is, against immigration from crowded world areas; policies regarding euthanasia, suicide and abortion; policies regarding the equalization of the roles of women and men in societal decision-making; policies regarding xenophobia. Moreover, the differences are too crucial to the current shaping of public and private policy to be set aside as purely academic or theoretical.

"If there is one trait which more than any other distinguishes *homo sapiens* from all other living creatures," Montagu says, "it is educability. Educability is the species trait of human-kind" (ibid., p. 11). According to Montagu, the special capacity for speech and the generalized capacity for problem-solving have been subject to the pressures of natural selection, but these pressures have resulted in a greater capacity to respond rather than merely to react. This capacity is what we call intelligence, and it is this capacity which generates the culture. He rejects Wilson's elimination of the voluntary as basic to culture-making and argues that the kind of brain that has genetically evolved permits voluntary rather than biologically-determined behavior. The brain is the organ of deliberation and choice.

On the particular issue of altruism, where Wilson looks to the naturalness of selfish behavior and emphasizes its pervasiveness, as do DeVore and Morris (1977), Montagu observes the naturalness of altruism, as does Fanon (1967). Montagu expresses this clearly:

> That altruistic behavior has a genetic basis I have not the least doubt. I have repeatedly set out the evidence for this, and it has recently been confirmed in babies and infants, whose altruistic behavior has long been known to some if not to others. What is, however, clear is that environmental factors play a decisive role in determining whether such behaviors will be developed or not (ibid., p. 7).

Montagu's assumption of a genetic base to altruism, juxtaposed with Wilson's assumption of genetically-controlled selfishness, provide the learning public with choices that lead to quite different political perspectives.[9] Montagu underscores this in discussing a study of scientists and their political beliefs: "Those holding conservative political views strongly tended to believe in the power of genes over environment. Those subscribing to more liberal views tended to believe in the power of environment over genes" (ibid., p. 4). The scholars agree on the centrality of altruism. They disagree on what it is and whence it originates. The special concern of sociologists of religion in this

debate is the influence of the different models on the interpretation of religious behaviors. For the established churches, the
consequences are immediate.

In the Christian tradition the commandment to love God
and the neighbor is explicitly extended to enemies and strangers
(Mt 5:43–48). Theologically speaking, this level of virtue can be
attained only with the help of God, by grace. The presence of
action, institutions and behaviors that manifest this disinterested
love toward strangers and enemies is the stated evidence of conversion won through redemption, itself presented as an act of
altruism. The evidence is in the giving of one's life for the other
who is not a member of the tribe, who is any stranger with a
need. Thus, in the Good Samaritan story, a man who is himself
an outcast goes beyond the generosity of the priest and the Lev-
ite, taking care of a stranger left for dead by the roadside and paying for his care; on his return later, after the healed stranger has
left, the altruist checks to see that those paid to do the service had
indeed carried it out (Lk 10:30–35).

On March 24, 1980, Archbishop Oscar Romero was gunned
down at the altar in El Salvador. Earlier, he had said of himself,
"A bishop will die but the church of God, which is the people,
will never perish" (Erdozain, p. 41). And again, "If God accepts
the sacrifice of my life, my hope is that my blood will be like a
seed of liberty and a sign that our hopes will soon become a reality" (ibid., p. 72). In an extended statement about his own death,
he said:

> My life has been threatened many times. I have to con-
> fess that, as a Christian, I don't believe in death without
> resurrection. If they kill me, I will rise again in the Sal-
> vadoran people. I'm not boasting or saying this out of
> pride, but rather as humbly as I can.
>
> As a shepherd, I am obliged by divine law to give
> my life for those I love, for the entire Salvadoran people,
> including those Salvadorans who threaten to assassi-
> nate me. If they should go so far as to carry out their
> threats, I want you to know that I now offer my blood
> to God for justice and the resurrection of El Salvador.

Martyrdom is a grace of God that I do not feel worthy of. But if God accepts the sacrifice of my life, my hope is that my blood will be like a seed of liberty and a sign that our hopes will soon become a reality (Interview recorded in a Mexican newspaper, *Excelsior*, in Erdozain, 1981, p. 75).

Romero's personal testimony indicates his readiness to give his life for the liberation of oppressed Salvadoran people who do not constitute an ethnic homogeneity. What they have in common is a Christian faith and a Latin American heritage of colonial experience with Western European and North American economic and political control. Romero was not acting in an idiosyncratic way when he took the pastoral positions expressed in his public statements but rather was giving evidence of his own conversion from a relatively conservative identification with state and economy, on the assumption that the social order was just, to a "preferential option for the poor," which was mandated by the Latin American bishops' conference in Medellín, Colombia in 1968 and reinforced ten years later in Puebla, Mexico (Eagleson and Scharper, 1979). Romero was the sixth priest to die for the liberation of the Salvadoran people between 1977 and 1980.

At the close of 1980, four North American women risked death for the same people: Maura Clark and Ita Ford, both Maryknoll missionaries; Dorothy Kazel, an Ursuline nun; and Jean Donovan, a lay missioner (Erdozain, 1981). All four returned to El Salvador knowing that they were risking their lives in doing so. They indicated their willingness to give their lives for the liberation of a people in the belief that this was a gospel mandate of the religion to which they had committed themselves, three by vow, one by a less formal choice. In eulogizing her colleagues, Sister Melinda Roper, president of Maryknoll, said:

The essential mystery of Jesus Christ is that he suffered, died, and rose to new life. He mandated us to solve the problems of suffering, to feed the hungry, clothe the naked, harbor the harborless, visit the sick, bury the dead.

These are not to be relegated to the realm of mystery, but to be solved; gospel issues, yes, but also political and economic (Maryknoll mimeograph).

The El Salvador drama was foreseen by theologian Edward Schillebeeckx, speaking at the Catholic University of Nijmegen in October 1978, concerning the CELAM conference to be held in Puebla, Mexico, the following January. He posed this question: "Does the Latin American church have the courage to confront the social-economic problems of the poor? And is it willing to risk 'being a sign of salvation for the world through solidarity with the poor in protest against poverty?' " (Schillebeeckx, 1980, p. 3). The question is posed in the words of the first formulation of liberation theology that arose out of the Latin American application of the Second Vatican Council (Gutiérrez, 1971). The problem of poverty in Latin America was formally addressed by Pope John XXIII in 1961 in an encyclical letter entitled *Christianity and Social Progress.* In it, he calls to account the Latin American bishops and, through them, the entire church of the continent for being too closely aligned with the established powers of the state and economy, to the neglect of the struggles of the poor. On top of this challenge came the Second Vatican Council and Pope Paul VI's letter, *The Development of Peoples.* In 1968, at Medellín, Colombia, the Latin American bishops responded by committing the church to a special "option for the poor."

In its formulation, the church's stand was strongly influenced by the educational method of Freire, the Brazilian educator exiled for his work in 1964. The method provided the model for what are called basic Christian communities, in which the poor of both rural and urban areas reflect on the conditions of their poverty and organize themselves to change those conditions (Freire, 1970; Lernoux, 1980; Libano, 1981). The "preferential option for the poor" also became the basis for a new form of theologizing which appeared with the publication of Gustavo Gutiérrez's *A Theology of Liberation* (1971). Since then, over five thousand books and articles have been published on the topic (Schillebeeckx, 1980, p. 4). According to Schillebeeckx:

The Medellín Conference demanded a "thoroughgoing, courageous, and radical renewal." The official church—not romantically but through dark experience—heard the cry of the Latin American people just as Yahweh heard his people's cry: "I have seen my people's affliction. . . . I know their sufferings . . ." (Ex 3:7–8). Medellín's final documents were not academic treatises that theorized as to whether the God of the Exodus has a precise societal analysis in mind. Opposing the ideology of economic growth as the basis for liberation, Medellín proclaimed the message of God's Kingdom and Jesus' predilection for people on society's boundaries. And what was true for Jesus is true also for Latin Americans: when one confronts the ideology of world power one gets killed. Medellín's spirit resulted in martyrs! This was the spirit that liberation theologians called to life (Schillebeeckx, 1980).

Schillebeeckx predicted the many deaths of church personnel two years prior to the death of Archbishop Romero but well after many other church personnel had died in the Latin American struggle for land for the poor. What he is saying is that Latin American theology, unlike European theology, is contextual in the sense that the conditions of the poor in the twentieth century call for a new reading of dogmatic and ethical issues. As Sobrino claims in *Christology at the Crossroads* (1978), a radical Christian critique of the conditions of the poor and a response to their cries leads not just to a change of heart but to a change of social and economic structures.

In theological language, the church becomes the visible sign of God's presence in and with the people and, to be this sign, it must break its connections with the world's powers (Schillebeeckx, p. 5). In this context, to maintain contact with and to support an unjust society is as political on the part of the church as it is to break that contact. Míguez-Bonino, theologizing from the Argentinian experience, sees European theology as a bourgeois affiliation grounded in nineteenth century idealism, a context that maintains the existing societal structure and the culture that supports it, while salvation history is essentially tied to a political liberation process (Míguez-Bonino, 1975).

Schillebeeckx's analysis of liberation theology, grounded as it is in a history that is happening, leaves him with the dilemma of how to affirm the radical action for the liberation of the poor and, at the same time, maintain the Christian rejection of the sacralization and absolutizing of politics—all the time recognizing that "keeping out of action" is itself a powerful political act. His problem as theologian parallels that of the sociologist studying churches in periods of social change. At the time he was writing, Schillebeeckx thought the Latin American bishops meeting in Puebla in 1979 would reject liberation theology, the basic Christian communities, conscientization, and the option for the poor. They did not. On the contrary, Puebla reaffirmed them (Comblin, 1980, p. 9). Sobrino explains how the final document formulated at the conference provides a theological rather than an ethical explanation of the "preferential option for the poor," going beyond a mandate to act to a biblical reflection on why and how that action for change is rooted in a theology of history (Sobrino, pp. 13–16). This analysis is useful to sociologists studying the relationship between religious belief and social behavior as a phenomenon separate from personal faith experiences.

The action of the Latin American church recounted here was not peculiar to the Catholic Church in Latin America during the past twenty years but is part of a worldwide church initiative recorded in the growing social justice and peace agenda of the Vatican Commission on Justice and Peace and the corresponding Justice and Service Unit of the World Council of Churches.[10] This action, in turn, is related to the development of the United Nations covenants on human rights and a movement within the Christian churches to stand with the poor of the world as they reach out to take what is rightfully theirs. It is a movement that began with the first formal response to workers' rights movements in the encyclical of Pope Leo XIII, *On the Conditions of the Working Class,* published in 1891. Gradually, that identification with the poor, even to the point of standing against the state when the state is characterized by organized injustice, has culminated at the present time in such actions as church officials calling on a National Guard not to obey orders to kill peasants who are doing what they have a right to do—that action that brought Archbishop Romero to his death in March 1980 (Erdozain, 1981, p. 79).

The study of this particular kind of altruism, which commits a role-player to an action on the basis of formal commitments to identify with a dispossessed segment of society, is the particular domain of the sociologist. Unlike the psychological studies of altruism that focus on personal motivation, these acts of giving up one's life can be predicted on the basis of a wider commitment made to fulfill the normative expectations of a newly-defined set of functions directly related to the authentic fulfillment of a traditional role.

There is evidence for this in the current research in which I am involved, concerning the changing structures of religious congregations of women. One major segment of it is the study of the revision of their constitutions. This study provides ample evidence of the possibility of predicting new behaviors from formally-adopted value commitments. A clear example of this relationship is evident in the constitutions of the Maryknoll Sisters, a group frequently featured in the news because of its altruistic risks while working with the poor in countries torn by civil wars. A single line from the constitutions predicts their actions in the light of their new understanding of their calling. They now define themselves as "women sent to be in solidarity with the poor not as an option but as a sign of the kingdom." Whether or not sociologists can yet see that these words mandate actions far different from what was earlier defined as the mission of religious women, the fact is that they predict behavior of an altruistic character. This behavior is oriented not to relatives, nor even to citizens of the same country, but, as in the case of this group, to a commitment to live and die among the poor of struggling third world nations—yes, and to be buried there also.

These behaviors are not explainable in individualistic terms. Social membership is a factor supporting the commitment when it is mandated by reason of values the group upholds. Whether or not the evidence of these acts of altruism challenges sociological and learning theories of altruism, grounded in assumptions of enlightened self-interest currently popular in social analysis, is not clear, but at the very least it provides a body of observations deserving serious examination and leading to quite different analyses and interpretations. The movement which aids established churches to stand with the poor against government structures that do not honor the human rights of the materially-dispossessed is a worldwide movement equal to, if not exceeding, the influence of the developing new religions which sociologists have spent considerable energy investigating and interpreting. Religious movements for structural change need this same serious consideration. Altruism has moved into central focus because affirming it as a social behavior calls for policy decisions quite contradictory to those that currently crowd the dossier of organizations with the power to influence the destiny of peoples. This is true in world perspective where decisions about trade, finance and migration are made, as well as at local levels dealing with the housing, education and health care of the working and non-working poor. Theories about altruism are simultaneously theories about religion.

Altruism as Public Virtue

The poor have moved to action. No longer are they passively awaiting the surplus of vital food and attention. All over the world they are taking stock of their lives, acting together and claiming their rights as human beings.

For those who want to deflect their demands and to justify their deaths or the deaths of those who join them in their struggle, one method is to label their efforts communistic or atheistic and then to enlist religion as a tool of resistance. It may at first seem puzzling that religion can be used both to stir up and to quell movements for justice—as when Christian Socialists were deposed by Christian Democrats in Chile in 1973—or that one Christian church can be organized against another—as has long been true in Northern Ireland and is true in Honduras today. But the religion whose central virtue is altruism has often been used to bestow a blessing on actions taken out of self-interest.

In biblical religion, Emmanuel (God with us) is the model of altruism; in Christianity, it is Jesus—who gave his life for the sinner, the stranger, the neighbor in need. The promise of his continued presence in the Eucharist is at the same time a promise that altruism—not just as a private virtue, but as a quality of community—is effective. That is the promise that has moved the faithful to announce to the poor the good news that they need be poor no longer. And the effect of that message has been that the poor, believing the biblical message, have taken social action aimed at claiming their rights as human beings (Cussianovich; Cardenal). This is the basis of the discovery by missionaries, reflected in a 1982 report by Dr. Jorge Lara-Brand, director of the Council on Theology of the Presbyterian Church of the U.S.A., that "the center of gravity in world Christianity has shifted to Africa and Latin America" and that the social justice agenda is the central emphasis of religion in the third world.[1]

Among those who are not poor, however, this shift in emphasis is often met with resistance and religion continues to be used as a tool of resistance. Religion is used by those with power to rally the patriotic and to nudge the reluctant to any public end that propaganda can justify. This is possible as long as self-interest is justified ethically as the fundamental premise of public policy. Wherever religion and patriotism are confused, biblical religion is compromised (R. Avila; Richard). Unlike the past, however, conditions today justify altruism as the practical as well as the ideal basis of public policy in advanced nations. While, for the poor, the good news is social justice, the same news demands an altruistic response on the part of the non-poor.

The good news today is that the poor are no longer doomed to illiteracy, thanks to social consciousness; no longer confined, like medieval serfs, to a vocabulary of six hundred words, thanks to mass media; no longer socially unaware, thanks to the mobility provided by new means of transportation and close contact with peers at work and school. The good news is that, thanks to labor unions and (for those who cannot get paying jobs) the United Nations human rights covenants, the poor need no longer accept a role as a reserve labor force, to be used at will and then discarded when technology enables a more efficient production of goods and services. Because of conscientization, they are no longer a *lumpen* proletariat. Together with others who experience hardship, like the elderly and the disabled, the poor can now be aware that they have human rights. Once organized, they experience power in having a voice and in sharing in group influence—including influence on non-poor altruists who, educated by the poor, are effective co-workers.

But altruism also needs organization if it is to be a dependable and consistent response to the just demands of the dispossessed and not just a transitory spasm of individual empathy. Altruism must be effectively incorporated into public policy. Its logical function is to displace self-interest, enlightened or otherwise, as the pragmatic basis of public policy. Self-interest, taken as a legitimate basis of public policy, seriously diminishes the human quality of those in non-poor nations and gives moral standing to the world's movement toward disaster. The poor are ready for citizenship in the world of nation-states. Conditions are now right for this passage.

The bad news is that the non-poor are now coming to be characterized by illiteracy, limited vocabulary, social unawareness and resistance to the just demands of the organized poor. Consequently, the educational challenge of our times is to fashion a pedagogy of the non-poor, rooted in education by the poor.[2] One international congregation of religious women, in the course of updating their constitutions in order to carry out the mission of the church (now changed by the emergence of the organized poor), has shaped a theology on which to base this new educational challenge. Theirs is a statement about where God is today. It reads:

> Inherent in our developing understanding of mission is the belief that God, who continues to speak to us in diverse ways, today calls to us with special insistence through the voices of the dispossessed and the materially poor as they attempt to organize themselves to claim their rights as human beings.[3]

Brazil provides evidence of the responsible development of the organized poor. The poor in that country were exposed in the early 1940's to the evangelizing done by young Christian workers and students exiled from France. Building on that experience, families in the rural northeast learned rapidly to read and write and also became politically aware, through the process known as conscientization. This began in the late 1950's. Through this program villagers addressed, in biblical perspective, repressive political, economic and social conditions and took organized action to change them (Freire, 1970).

Facilitators for this teaching method were reinforced by the powerful *Mater et Magistra*, promulgated by Pope John XXIII in

1961 (O'Brien, pp. 44–116). The encyclical buttressed the efforts of those helping poor farm families build "basic Christian communities" in which the gospel message is applied to the task of changing the unjust conditions of their lives. They again received support from the institutional church with the issuance of John XXIII's *Pacem in Terris* in 1963 (O'Brien and Shannon, pp. 117–170). In 1967, the publication of the United Nations human rights covenants and the World Council of Churches' Uppsala Conference here matched by Pope Paul VI's *Populorum Progressio* (*The Development of Peoples*). Meanwhile, the documents of the Second Vatican Council recognized as practical and holy the effort to put science and technology at the service of human development. Finally, in various ecumenical initiatives (SODEPAX) and in conferences of Catholic bishops at Medellín in 1968 and Puebla in 1979, social action on the part of the poor and the theology that grew from it were seen to have come of age (Brown; Eagleson and Scharper).

Simultaneously with developments in Latin America came the demands by colonized African peoples that they be recognized as sovereign peoples. They met with resistance from the colonial nations, however, which only reluctantly relinquished the control they had enjoyed over education—a control exercised mainly through religion—and allowed the African peoples to promote their own literacy and public health programs (Appiah-Kubi; Cabral).

As in the Asian struggle in Vietnam, action for social justice in Guinea-Bissau, Tanzania, Angola and Mozambique was quickly defined as communist, with the implication that it was atheistic and evidence of the growing power of the Soviet Union. Newly-conditioned by television advertising and classroom textbooks, now published by transnational corporations, the non-poor responded without much compassionate analysis to the stimuli of consumerism. They reacted against the organizing poor as dangerous aliens, allied with the Soviet Union or Cuba, an alliance portrayed as so inherently evil as to justify violent resistance and the threat of nuclear force.

The rapid development of literacy in rural third world areas should have been an impetus to those who tried to teach reading in the inner-city areas of the United States. Instead, we in the United States asserted the right of the CIA to help overthrow, in 1964, the Brazilian government that had supported the church-related literacy program there. When the poor in Chile, abetted by organized workers, tried to replace a Christian capitalist government with a Christian socialist government in 1973, the U.S. again collaborated in the violent overthrow of the elected leaders, and that despite the fact that the Chilean initiative was guided by Christian social teaching and the methods of conscientization affirmed by the Medellín conference of bishops in 1967.

The violent overthrow of the Allende government appeared legitimate to many of us in the United States, not only to protect United States copper interests but also to support the definition of Chile as an atheistic communist country. Current military and political interventions in Central America, and their interpretation in the news media, are further evidence of a growing insensitivity to the poor as they struggle for access to the resources they need. The specter of communist association is easily conjured up, basically because our national self-interest is served by opposition both to the Soviet Union and to third world liberation movements.

The poor, whose "natural inadequacies" once obliged us in charity to reach out and help, are now "dangerous revolutionaries" competing for resources we assume to be too scarce to meet their needs as well as our own. Action against them is justified by the need to protect U.S. interests (Chomsky). Justified, for example, are the high interest rates on International Monetary Fund loans—loans that deepen the debt and the dependency of developing nations. As long as the poor remain unorganized, whether they be third world peoples or minorities in the first world, we define them as the "white man's burden" and respond with charity. Once organized, they are held to the rules of fair exchange, as if they were equals in power and wealth. We then feel justified in pitting our self-interest against theirs—this, fundamentally, on the now dated assumption that people are too plentiful and goods too scarce to meet the needs of all.

Educational materials published by the Population Reference Bureau have shown since 1980 that world population is not on an endless upward curve but is leveling off and will probably stabilize at about 10.5 billion around the year 2110.[4] The 1983 World Population Data Sheet shows that the index of sufficiency of food, defined as per capita calorie supply as a percentage of requirement, is 109 percent—134 percent for the developed world, 99 percent for the developing.

What those figures show is that the more-developed nations, which make up 25 percent of the world population, stand a high chance of being overfed, while the less-developed world, 53 percent exclusive of China, do not have enough food to stay alive and well. But, more than that, they show that there is more than enough food for everyone. The root of the problem is laid bare in a 1980 United Nations analysis:

> If all the food that is produced in the world could be equitably distributed there would be more than enough for everyone. Instead we have a paradox: more food is being produced today than ever before and more people are hungry than ever before. . . . The problem lies in the imbalance of the world economy which leaves large numbers of people without the money to pay for food which is plentiful (United Nations, 1980, p. 45).

One further datum is necessary to set the issue of non-scarcity in its proper frame. In 1981, U.S. Secretary of Agriculture John R. Block warned farmers that "they will not be eligible for Government loans and subsidies next year unless they reduce the number of acres they normally plant in wheat" (*New York Times*, July 11, 1982, p. 16). A month later, a *New York Times* caption over a huge bin of corn read, "Farmers Once Again Growing Too Much Corn To Eat and Sell" (Aug. 15, 1982, p. 8E). In April 1983, the *New York Times* reported that the farmers had yielded, with the result that "the depressed farm futures markets suddenly came to life early last month in a burst of price gains, volume and open interest." "The reason," the newspaper reported, "is that a surprisingly large number of farmers have signed up for the Government's payment-in-kind program, which is aimed primarily at reducing the huge grain surpluses and bolstering farm prices" (*New York Times,* April 4, 1983, p. D9).

This report, on just one series of decisions that characterize U.S. national policy, demonstrates that scarcity then is defined not in terms of felt hunger but in terms of money to pay. Limiting concern to survival of U.S. farmers and the money market is assumed to be normal. East Africa, West Africa, and now Southern Africa need that wheat; so do North and South Yemen, Afghanistan, Bangladesh, India, Cambodia, East Timor, Laos, Vietnam, El Salvador, Guatemala, and Honduras, as well as Haiti and the Dominican Republic. All these countries cannot feed themselves with what they are now able to produce.

Cuba does not need the wheat; it produces 117 percent of the food it needs for all its citizens to have a balanced diet. Twenty years ago, Cuba was as poor as Haiti. Today, life expectancy there is 72, two years below that of the U.S., while Haiti's is still 52. But it is Haiti's people who capsize off our affluent coast, while we continue to root our policies in the assumption of the "lifeboat" ethic—in the belief that, if we let them in, our boats will sink also, and we will all die.

Why are *we* and *they* defined by Christians in national terms, just as they were by tribes in ancient times and by the city-states of Greece, each of which had its own household and city gods? Those were tribal and pagan times. On what basis can a national policy be based on self-interest and claim to be Christian? And even if "the people" could be so narrowly defined in the past, why does that definition persist today, when we have to create artificial scarcity and when, barring planned obsolescence, we have the technology to provide enough food for the world's people (World Resource Institute; Murphy, 1983, 1984, 1985)? On a different premise, we could use our technological skills to create an economy that would provide for all. With our science and technology we could create durable goods and convert worn-out material to serviceable new material. Instead, we increasingly produce weapons useful only to destroy people and the earth itself, because our economic policy is still rooted in a false assumption of scarcity, and our public policy, in self-interest.

Current estimates of people per square kilometer of arable

land, food and energy production, and available minerals all suggest that, with planning and will, providing for human need is not beyond a technical solution. It is a question of social motivation, of political and economic choices about who controls the world's resources (George; World Resource Institute).

While overall world population growth is declining—and the rate of decline is steep in Oceania, North America, the Soviet Union and Japan—the rate is still increasing in Latin America, Africa and Asia, at least in the short run. The rate of population change is linked inversely with per capita gross national product. Birth rates decline as infant survival and life-expectancy rise. The problem is that where 70 percent of the world's people live, only 30 percent of the wealth is available. They are the world's progeny. As first world peoples, we need to prepare ourselves to let them have what they need and come where there is room to live.

Sociologists analyzing the role of religion in society have often found it supporting, reinforcing, even celebrating, the nation-state. Many theorists have seen that as its only intended function, as if religion were equivalent to patriotism, and their analysis of religion is restricted to its reinforcing role (Richard; Durkheim). Studies have focused on local, especially ethnic, churches in America, to see to what extent they preserved old ethnic ties or became channels of Americanization (Winter; Lenski). When the churches confronted civil rights issues, other studies revealed that Christians opted for money and members rather than social justice (Pettigrew and Campbell). An emphasis on invisible religion later allowed the churches' social ethic to maintain its personal focus (Berger and Luckman). Current studies on the new religions of the political right demonstrate further how easily religion is linked with the special interests of existing states. Much of the research, in fact, seems centrally concerned with the question of how dependable religious consciousness is as a buttress of public order.

The ease with which churches can be coopted in the interests of nation, race and class is illustrated by the history of the national churches, like the Anglican, Greek and Russian Orthodox, Dutch Reformed, and Catholic in Spain and Portugal, which carried colonial culture to India, the Middle East, China, Africa,

Latin America and South Africa. There is the same attempt to co-opt religion in the U.S. today.

The Catholic Church played a role in the U.S. intervention in Vietnam as it does today in Central America, where major church figures can be found on both sides of the liberation efforts. Churches play a role in the Middle East, Southeast Asia and Northern Ireland. Church influence is sought to establish public policy—even when that policy is manifestly at odds with nations and peoples whose survival church doctrine purports to support. The alignment of churches with the national interest—while church ministry is said to be properly concerned with purely spiritual matters—is a political act that deserves serious and honest research (Varacalli).

Increasingly, however, church activity is taking the side of oppressed peoples against state interests. In their official capacity as teachers and ethical guides, churches are teaching their members and the general public that the biblical message is not one of national self-interest but of human rights, rights that are to be honored even unto death. The deaths of Archbishop Romero and four American women in El Salvador in 1980 prompted American church bodies, acting through the National Council of Churches and the National Conference of Catholic Bishops, to stand officially with them, altruists who gave their lives for the people. Many church officials saw their actions as biblically rooted.

However, much of the public and some church officials judged them as communists—that is, as atheistic—and found that the use of violence against them was warranted. Whence comes the idea that what is not in the national interest is not in God's interest? Why, when the National and World Councils of Churches supported the struggles of African peoples, were they defined by their members and by *60 Minutes* as communists or dupes of communists? Why did the Catholic bishops' pastoral letter on war and peace so divide that body?

We sometimes shrug off these divisions as political, not religious, ascribing them to human weaknesses masquerading under the guise of religion. But while religions can be lured into supporting national and personal self-interest (Dawson, 1948), they can also challenge that selfishness. When the gospel is re-read in view of current data about population and resources, two distinct messages are revealed, one for the poor and one for the non-poor (Senior and Stuhlmueller; Gottwald; Gutiérrez, 1983). For the poor, the good news is that the land belongs to them (Lev 25). For the non-poor, it is that God will not abandon them as they release their grip on the things poor people need to survive (Ont 6; Neal, 1977). Liberation theology spells out the good news for the poor (Gutiérrez; Míguez-Bonino; Cone; Ruether; Támez). A first world response is in the making (Brown), but it is also meeting resistance (Novak). What is needed is a social ethic grounded both in liberation theology and in a corresponding theology of relinquishment.

Sociologists provide an historical explanation of this point. Introducing their *Varieties of Civil Religion*, Robert Bellah and Phillip Hammond observed in 1980:

> In the formative period of the American republic a vigorous public philosophy complemented our public theology. It justified a strong normative concern for the common good that was implied in the symbolism of the differentiated civil religion. But public philosophy faded with the founding generation. It was largely replaced by the overwhelmingly private philosophy of liberalism, which justified public action exclusively on the grounds of private interest. The common good was expressed in religious terms or not at all. Fitful expressions of public philosophy have occurred in our history, most notably in the twentieth century in the work of John Dewey, but no continuous tradition has developed. At the moment when religious symbols are more and more co-opted by ultraconservatives and the philosophy of liberalism seems less and less adequate as a guide to our public or private lives, a revival of public philosophy seems urgently needed (1980, p. xiv).

If politics is the art of the possible, and social ethics the pragmatic application of how to be good within those possibilities, then it would seem logical and feasible—given an adequate food supply, a tapering population, and an already-existing world economy of transnational corporations—that an ethic be devised based on the disinterested love of those in need. It will be an ethic of altruism rather than of self-interest, centered in human caring rather than in rules of fair play. It will call for a network of human commitment rather than a hierarchy of command and control. With a new division of labor between men and women in the Church, such an ethic could be developed there on the basis of experience. From there, it can move into the public sector.

◆ VI

Social Justice and the Right To Use Power

It was 1958 and the issue was the integration of Hall High School in Little Rock, Arkansas. It was an issue on which all Christian churches, at the level of their national organizations, had taken a clear position: segregation was a sin. For various reasons, however, local churches were resisting integration.

At the time, I was a graduate student in the sociology department at Harvard, studying the analysis of social data in a course taught by Samuel Stouffer. On the question of how Little Rock ministers would respond to the mandates to integrate handed down by their national organizations, we hypothesized that those who were secure enough would cooperate.

Events were to prove us wrong. Our study showed that questions of money and members took precedence over national church directives and that secure ministers, in charge of churches and enjoying relatively permanent appointments, were the most resistant to integration. We also found, however, that a number of ministers without that security risked their careers by supporting the integration effort.

We did not follow their careers, nor did we assess the power and authority of the national church bodies' consensus on integration. Having shown that churches can be coopted in the interests of wealth, power and security, we felt our work was done. Thomas Pettigrew and Ernest Campbell, authors of *Christians in Racial Crisis*, were post-doctoral fellows in the course, as were Daniel Levinson, author of *The Authoritarian Personality*, Irwin Sanders, a specialist in East European peasant cultures, and

Neil Smelser, who studied society and the economy. There were only fifteen of us in the course and all of us, from our different religious perspectives, were disturbed by the findings.

We were all white, and all had studied with Gordon Allport. In his *The Nature of Prejudice,* Allport found that, although regular churchgoers express more racial prejudice than non-church-goers, churchgoers who are familiar with the beliefs of their churches are not only more likely than non-churchgoers to be free of prejudiced behavior and opinion but more willing to act in the interests of a stranger in need.

Wanting to find out more about the relationship between be-lief in God and acting for social justice, I chose as my doctoral dissertation to study the beliefs and behaviors of priests in the archdiocese of Boston, who were under pressure to support causes aimed at changing behavior that violated social justice principles. My findings suggested that what distinguished their responses was not so much the degree of their belief in God but whether they experienced God as, on the one hand, remote, out-side the world, and acting over people or, on the other, imma-nent, involved in the world, and acting through people. The study was published as *Values and Interests in Social Change* and provided the framework of a twenty-year study of the changing structure of Catholic congregations of women in the United States (Neal, 1965).

In 1968, when I was teaching in the sociology department of the University of California at Berkeley, two of the students in a seminar I was conducting were leaders in a strike of graduate as-sistants which was aimed at drawing university attention to the movement of third world peoples. One was helping research fac-ulty and students to determine the background of those whose academic interests had turned to third world liberation. These students went into the mountains on weekends to pray and, in interviewing them, I developed the items I needed to discrimi-nate between people who contemplate and those who do not—items essential for a study of contemplative orders of men and women, and which had not been successfully formulated from interviewing the contemplatives themselves. Although the stu-dents had provided the valid items to measure contemplation, they had been described in the media as dangerous, subversive, atheistic secularists. The fact that some principals in the movement were deeply religious was barely presented to the public: it did not fit the image of the dissidents that those who opposed the liberation movement wanted to present.

Doubting the holiness of those who struggle for human liberation continues to characterize public policy. On December 2, 1980, four Catholic women, three of them members of religious communities and one a lay volunteer, were raped and murdered in El Salvador by members of the National Guard. Within twenty-four hours the U.S. representative to the United Nations suggested on national television that they must have been subversives, and the Secretary of State, also on national television, called them gun-runners. A carefully documented television story, *Roses in December*, prepared by Maryknoll as the result of untiring efforts by brothers of two of the victims, revealed the women's authentic religious commitment. What prompted them to work for, and if necessary die for, the liberation of a manifestly exploited people in Central America was a commitment to altruism rooted in deep religious belief. But because investigating the causes of their deaths violated the national interest, the judgment of the justice of their cause remains hidden in State Department records.

All biblical religions affirm the liberation of peoples. In practice, however, there are limits on those designated as people. The poor or the dispossessed are defined instead as enemies, as less than human, as children rather than responsible adults, or as incompetent and thus in need of care. So defined, the poor need not be taken seriously when they challenge the right of those in power to use that power to suppress their human rights.

As long as people worshiped tribal gods, the gods were counted on to protect the tribe. With the concept of one God came the concept of one people. From that perspective, any ethnic co-optation of God is recognized as a retribalization—or what we now call the nationalization—of religion. In the biblical context, to equate love of country with the love of God is recognized as idolatry. In that circumstance, religious restraints are not applicable to the state's treatment of foreigners who are not members of friendly nations (Richard et al.). Similarly, when religion becomes aligned with the interests of a class, the rest of the people are not included in the community of the faithful or among those enjoying the protection of the law. The nineteenth century discovery by workers of that betrayal by the churches was a grave scandal. The decision by some organized workers to look elsewhere for salvation was a judgment on the churches' class-identification. A study of the religious response of the church to that judgment by workers promises to yield evidence of the role of religion in societal transformation and to help us understand current world struggles for the survival and development of peoples.[1]

In modern industrial societies, power rests on five bases: control over land, labor, industry and trade, over the unknown—especially the terrifying unknown—and over violence. People who exercise these controls participate in decision-making; where they are concentrated in the hands of one group, there is dictatorship (Barrington Moore). In ancient and feudal times, when control over land and labor, in the form of slaves and serfs, was the principal basis of power, the idea of God as provident father provided for the peasants a channel of liberation. With urban industrial development, producers and traders became more powerful but workers came to reflect on the injustice of their working and living conditions and the labor union enabled them to organize to press their demands for justice. In 1891 the Catholic Church affirmed their right to do so.[2] But not until the late twentieth century, with the United Nations movement for a New International Economic Order (1974), did those with no control over production in their own countries find reason to hope that industry and trade could provide for their needs.

Universal education was the first step toward people's winning effective control over the unknown. Literacy readied people not only for humanistic reflection but for scientific inquiry and social analysis. For workers, this became possible when literacy became essential for effective production. Through conscientization, dispossessed peoples gained access to words and learned to make new words to analyze their experience, to become aware of the political, social and economic causes of their oppression, and to act to change the oppressive conditions (Freire, p. 19). It extended the range of their reflective action beyond the exigencies of their hungry village. In the process, many of the poor have come to understand why education was not extended to them in the past and why, for example, the white population in South Africa gets free books and tuition while the black population, 72 percent of the people, have to pay for theirs.

The power of weapons, especially nuclear weapons, already stockpiled in quantities sufficient to destroy the world and still being produced, makes this the basic social justice issue today. Who if anyone has the right to use these weapons? Control over violence is today the major determinant of power although, as the news blackout during the 1983 invasion of Grenada by U.S. forces illustrates, control of the unknown can enhance a government's power to use violence. That is because, by controlling the unknown, the shared definition of a situation can be limited to the perspective of those in power.

In earlier times, control of the unknown was the prerogative of religious role players, because God and the devil alone dwelt beyond the village. In early modern times, they shared that power with scientists. Now, given the advanced technology of telecommunications, much of that power has moved to the owners and controllers of the media. To learn about aspects of a situation masked by the media, people need to hear from the victims. The United Nations provides a voice for the smaller nations but, even there, the vote is controlled by the United States and the Soviet Union, the nations with the most control over the use of violence.

As Weber demonstrated in *The Protestant Ethic and the Spirit of Capitalism,* the human energy required initially in the move from feudalism to capitalism came from religious enthusiasm. In the northern hemisphere, any movement away from capitalism is still associated with atheism in public opinion. Studies of the electronic church, for example, suggest that its adherents are so strongly pro-capitalist and anti-communist that any consideration of a different international economic ordering is inevitably defined in their media as communistic or atheistic.

The advent of an era of high technology in telecommunications means we can understand more about the efforts of third world peoples to develop. Alternatively, that information can be selectively excluded, either by the equipment itself or by the management of information for which social psychology now provides the skills (Martin). It all depends on whether information is available through channels designed to serve the interest of the people or whether the leaders of trade and industry collaborate with government to control access to information in their own interests.

The basic human right of a people to self-determination, formulated in 1967 in the U.N. International Bill of Rights, goes beyond law. In a thirteenth century treatise—dealing not with self-actualizing but with survival needs (Blanchette)—Thomas Aquinas declared that "in cases of need all things are common property, so that there would seem to be no sin in taking another's property, for need has made it common."[3] The Second Vatican Council reactivated that thesis in its Pastoral Constitution on the Church in the Modern World: "If one is in extreme necessity, he has the right to procure for himself what he needs out of the riches of others" (#69). Other church documents extend that right to whole peoples, sanctioning liberation movements of third world peoples throwing off the yoke of colonialism and imperialism—*The Development of Peoples*, 1967; Pope Paul VI's letter, *Call to Action*, 1971; the document of the bishops' synod, Call to Action, 1971 (O'Brien). In its Uppsala meeting of 1967 and in several journal documents and monographs in the 1970's, the World Council of Churches provided similar guidelines (SODEPAX). The documents have earned for both church bodies the label of communist.

Reflection on the struggle of third world countries, as well as on these documents, has given rise to liberation theologies, including those originating in Latin America and Africa (Gutiérrez; Míguez-Bonino; Támez; Basil Moore; Appiah-Kubi; Torres), those developed by women (Ruether; Fiorenza), and by black theologians in the U.S. (Cone). Beyond declaring them to be too political for religious role players, little systematic study has been done of their influence on modern liberation movements. Ac-

customed by political indoctrination to associate liberation movements with the Soviet Union or Cuba, societies whose peoples
we conclude are not free, few scientists devote themselves to the
systematic study of liberation in its religious aspect, concentrat-
ing only on its political and secularizing aspects.

One aspect of the link between religion and society that
needs careful study is the difference in people's ideas about God
and where God is to be found, depending on whether they are
bent on liberation or on repressing movements of liberation. The
image of God as a father in heaven, with the family of man as his
children, does not describe the experience of blacks in South Africa or women in most societies (Ntwasa; Daly, 1973). The lack
of fit between the patriarchal model of God and their own experience leads some to reject religion, especially if those who
control access to religious roles will not allow any other symbol
of God to compete with the father image.

But others will search for new symbols of God as part of the
practice of their religion and their pursuit of justice (Russell;
Ruether, 1983). As long as society wants to keep the oppressed
in their traditional place, those who control religious symbols can
use the tradition to deny legitimacy to the pursuit of new symbols. Conversely, as the poor begin organizing to claim their
rights, ideas about God change radically. In Nicaragua, for example, the traditional church divides, and divides at the highest
levels of its authority, over the support it will give to the beliefs
of the organized poor (Cabestrero). But the most basic division
is that which sunders the poor and the non-poor from one another, even as they worship as members of the same church.
When that happens, who has the right to use power over whom?
(Gutiérrez, 1983; Hanks; Herzog).

The right to use power is authority. In his insightful analysis
Weber recognized three bases for authority, all of them rooted in
the fact that the right to use power is given by those over whom
or with whom it is exercised. For Weber, authority is given (1) to
the charismatic person, to whose commands the people are responsive, (2) to tradition, when those who believe in the tradition agree to limit their and others' behavior to that which
accords with the tradition, and (3) to law, which replaces charism

and tradition when people enjoying relative equality agree to obey the law rather than be fined, imprisoned, or killed (Weber, 1937). Sociologists usually find these three bases of authority—charism, tradition, and law—sufficient to account for the different ways in which people accord to others the right to use power, either by cooperating in its use or at least not resisting it.

When minorities are exploited under the law, or third world peoples find that the laws protecting foreign property rights prevent their using their own lands to feed and shelter their own people, the question arises of whether there is any other basis for restricting the rights of some to exercise power over others. Under South Africa's program of apartheid, for example, a people experiences control by others under laws that do not protect their basic human rights. When charism, tradition, and law are not appropriate foundations for the right to use power, then, is there any other foundation? Is there any new development of authority that is peculiar to the present and in need of scientific analysis? One answer may be found in organized religion's new and vigorous support of human rights.

Historically, when the poor gained access to real power (as in some European political parties of the nineteenth and early twentieth century), they "left the church." The phenomenon was interpreted as part of a process of secularization, as if liberation movements were naturally atheistic. Even where the poor have grown to understand their rights in the course of biblical reflection and in liturgical settings (Cardenal), and seek God's aid in their dangerous venture, their struggle for power is often defined even now as a forsaking of religion for politics. But religion is never apolitical, and the drift of the organized poor from patriarchal churches may simply reflect the fact that, as they experience a measure of power, they no longer find in those churches a credible image of God.

Studying religion in international perspective permits an analytic distinction between religion and patriotism. Whether religious or irreligious, a person is a citizen, a member of a social class, politically active within more or less organized groups, groups which more or less shape his or her vision of what is right, good, useful and possible. But this vision does not exhaust the concept of religion as such. Social scientists and psychologists have well examined the political uses of religion but we cannot afford to leave off further research just because our own class interests are satisfied, especially when new data need to be taken into account.

Our operating ethical systems rest on certain assumptions about scarcity and over-population, including the assumption that world population increase is geometrically outstripping the available food supply. Current statistics call these assumptions into question. So far the only large-scale U.S. response to the problems of abundance and hunger has been to limit food production to what can be sold to or eaten by those who are already overfed.

Two economic systems, capitalist and communist, currently compete for world domination. Capitalism is treated positively in studies of religion; communism is treated negatively. Within capitalist economies, the U.N. covenants that protect political and civil rights are affirmed; within communist economies those that protect economic and cultural rights—including the rights to food, clothing, shelter, education, health care, social security, and to organize the workplace—are affirmed. The result is that local churches in the first world still tend to support a form of economic development that clearly cannot permit third world countries to care for their people. A third world country like Cuba, which has managed to raise the life-expectancy of its people to within two years of the United States, is rejected here. So, until very recently, was China, which has done almost as well over thirty years and which contains one-fifth of the world's people. Moreover, when people in a third world country choose socialism, even in one of its various Christian forms, there is a tendency to classify them as atheistic communists. Religion may then be used to condition public opinion to the use of violence against them—as in Nicaragua, Chile, Brazil, Angola, Tanzania, Mozambique, and Grenada.

How can we support the government of South Africa when it denies political and civil rights to 72 percent of its people and exerts control over Namibia but claims, in doing so, that it is a Christian state? The position of our government is that we will continue to support South Africa as long as Cubans are in Angola, because Angola is inimical to our national self-interest. By what authority does the United States use power to delay the independence of Namibia until its conditions are met?

In world perspective it is clear that religion is more than a political tool for powerful nations to use against liberation movements. For one thing, those who are struggling to assert their human rights readily turn to religious groups for support, groups which are likely to respond, more or less effectively, because of their beliefs and their commitment to altruism. In our concern to keep control over the violence of popular liberation movements, it is easy to lose sight of the religious energy moving people to reach out and take what is theirs even as it moves others to let them have what they need for survival.

In a world in which there are resources enough to meet the needs of all, movements inspired by religion can be effective for achieving social justice. First world people often define liberation movements as atheistic, and so stiffen resistance to them, because of fear of control by powers that limit access to the unknown and threaten violent destruction. But we live with these fears anyway. With new models for investigating theism and atheism—concerned less for who God is than for where God is found—our imaginations could be freed to consider new forms of economic development.

VII

Education for Justice

Education never takes place in a vacuum. It is always a function of a political and economic system. Because social justice is a measure of how well such systems meet human needs, education plays a key role in social justice concerns. Three sociological theories help define that role.

First, functional sociology teaches that people will rally around programs and policies to the extent that those programs and policies reflect shared values (Parsons), values that are articulated in education, religious institutions, and in family life. Second, conflict theory demonstrates that there are values that act—through cultural channels like art, literature, music, and sports—to maintain the existing distribution of power, wealth and prestige (Barrington; Moore; Maduro; Otten). Third, as symbolic interaction theory shows, people construct reality in social interaction. If myths generated to preserve our interests are believed to be real, they are real in their consequences.[1]

Education, according to this theory, need have little to do with truth. Its role is to train a new generation to perceive the world through the myths and structures already in place. Those assigned to teach, given access to effective channels of communication, foster the learning that keeps the system going. For this purpose, teachers use materials designed to mesh with consumer interests fanned by advertising and by materials provided by publishing companies which are often owned by transnational companies (Collins and Makowsky, p. 243; Otten, p. 201).

How we, as citizens of the world's wealthiest nation, see our choices depends on the values we share. A key to our values lies in the answer we give, personally and collectively, to the question of how many people there are in our community. If we take seriously the right of peoples "to enjoy and utilize fully and freely their natural wealth and resources" (United Nations, 1978), the only acceptable answer to that question is 5 billion, the number of people currently inhabiting the planet.

Because the human family seems too large, however, and because it is so fragmented, there are many ideologies, theories and policies in place to legitimate a tighter definition of the community, a definition that, in leaving some outside, marks them for elimination. A wish like that will need to be masked, if we value human life and development, by theories of a natural law of self-interest and the justice of hoarding scarce resources (Lewontin). When people narrow their interests to the survival and well-being of a community that is much smaller than the 5 billion who make up the world's population, education is harnessed to fit those narrowed interests. Facts which contradict the chosen definition of reality may not even appear in the curriculum (Neal, 1965). These include the potential leveling-off of world population at 10.5 billion around 2110, the adequacy of the world's food, energy and mineral resources to provide for a world community of that size (Murphy), the recognition by the United Nations of peoples' rights to self-determination (United Nations, 1978), and the worldwide move by the church toward support of poor people as they gather in basic Christian communities to assert their human rights (Dorr; R.M. Brown; Schillebeeckx, 1979; LADOC).

What these facts indicate is the need for a thorough revamping of the structures and policies currently in place for producing and distributing goods and services, and a challenging of the assumptions that underlie our choices to produce weapons and to curtail production of food (*New York Times*, Aug. 15, 1982, p. E8). Typical is the device that held up emergency aid to drought-stricken Central Africa in April 1984—when five million people were dying of starvation—by attaching the Weiss Bill (H.R. 4863) as a rider requiring the shipment of arms to El Salvador. When our basic values and assumptions are tied to national self-inter-

est, a self-interest defined in terms of maintaining corporate in-
vestment and trading partnerships, altruism is sacrificed to
destructive impulses. This kind of choice is abetted by narrow
use of the social sciences and outmoded ethical and philosophical assumptions about human nature, rights and responsibilities.
From the perspective of the Judaic-Christian ethic, it is of no negative consequence that in the not too distant future the world's
people will be predominantly of African, Asian and Latin American background. From the perspective of any humanistic value
system, in fact, the racial composition of our progeny is of little
concern, yet it continues to operate as a negative factor in national policy.

The fact is that a considerable measure of racism informs our
decisions about whom we accept as colleagues and peers and
whom we relegate to servant status. One need only examine the
services provided for racially different peoples in cities throughout the United States, our selective treatment of new immigrants, and our efforts to control peoples newly liberated or
struggling for liberation in Latin America, Africa, and Southeast
Asia. Accepting as our progeny all the world's people is a real-
izable value that could be implemented now in the way we educate our children and re-educate ourselves. But is that what we
really want to do?

Providing sufficient goods and services is a new human possibility. With available technology, it is possible to provide more,
and more durable, goods and at the same time save resources by
recycling them. In using that capital-intensive technology, furthermore, there would be plenty of unemployed workers eager
to provide labor-intensive services to those who, due to illness,
age, ignorance or disability, need one-on-one care or small-
group interaction to develop their human potential. But it seems
difficult to determine how to finance this new division of labor,
with fewer people in industry and clerical work and more in human services. Ideas about financing are caught up in a mystique
of market systems committed to maximizing profits, and including a concept of human nature shaped by premises of natural
self-interest.

Given such premises, we feel justified in limiting our caring, extending it sometimes only to our families, sometimes to our ethnic group, sometimes even to the nation—but seldom, if ever, to the world. On such premises we concur in bureaucratic decisions uncontrolled by value frameworks, decisions that lead to the destruction of environments and peoples, even of ourselves. It is a logic buttressed by a belief that God sanctions the destruction of some peoples, on account of their supposed atheism. It is a logic that leads to the bureaucratization that created nazism, fascism, and communism (Mannheim; Michels).

We could be more effective by developing models of the practice of participatory decision-making on the part of the workers who produce goods and services and on the part of neighborhood peoples planning for the housing and human services they need. Some write off these models as utopian but, when poor peoples learn to participate in making the decisions that affect them and become literate and effective in the process (Freire), we destroy them as enemies (Cardenal; de Castro; Brother John of the Weston Priory; Schillebeeckx). We caricature theologies that mandate the participatory model (Novak); we exile the educator who develops an effective method of literacy (Freire); we attribute the success of democratic Christian Socialism, even when it is obviously the fruit of local initiative, to the machinations of atheistic communists brought in from Russia and Cuba (Eagleson); and organizers we define as atheistic or communist we feel justified in killing (Erdozain; Berryman).

These socially-constructed realities are class-limited, racist, and tailored to culturally conceived self-interest. But they are not natural. The limitations we put on human nature, and our choice of scholars to provide theoretical justification for our choices, dividing the world into *us* and *them*, stem from our fear that if *they* had access to scarce resources they would exclude us just as we now exclude them.

In our selfish planning we have generated a monster, the arms race, capable of destroying them and us alike. But value-based action can prevent this. It is possible to reconceptualize the human condition and, on that basis, plan a course of action that meets the needs of the whole human family. Human development is a matter of human choice, a technically solvable problem.

If we lack the vision or will to solve the inherent problems of social organization, it is because we are caught up in erroneous conceptions about human nature and about the supposedly aggressive instincts and ungovernable psychic energies of peoples different from ourselves.

The evidence is that populations decline in rate of growth as they come to control the resources they need for development. In world meetings, third world nations argue for development funds and for a right to participate, not just as consultants but as peers, in charting the course of their development (United Nations, 1974, 1980). In calling for a "fundamental reordering of the basic values and priorities of economic development," the Canadian Conference of Bishops provided a guide for the inclusion of peoples in planning their own futures (Baum and Cameron, p. 15).

This considered request is for a planned economy that does not entail the loss of human freedom as the price of food, shelter, and clothing. In the West there is the scandal of accumulation of private wealth, the neglect of human services to the unemployed, and reliance on a military build-up now capable of destroying the world. In the East the scandal is one of limited human freedom. Both East and West violate third world nations' rights of self-determination, either by invasion or by arms and trade agreements. Third world demands stem from the belief that security and freedom are not mutually exclusive and that the idea that they are derives from elite ideologies designed to preserve a status quo in which North America, Europe, Japan, and the Soviet Union, containing 25 percent of the world's peoples, control 75 percent of its resources.

The conflicting definitions of human rights in East and West are reflected in the two covenants that make up the United Nations Bill of Rights, adopted as international law in 1976, and indeed are the reason that there are two covenants instead of one. The Covenant on Civil and Political Rights, with its guarantees of freedom, was easily affirmed in the West. The Covenant on Economic, Social, and Cultural Rights, more concerned with guarantees of material well-being, was easily affirmed in the East. The West provides for liberty and makes a commodity of material well-being; the East provides for material well-being and withholds liberty. Third world peoples seek both.

Which set of rights seems of most pressing concern depends on where people are in their progress toward development. Poor people, for whom the immediate need is simply to stay alive, are concerned primarily with the second set of rights; non-poor people are in a position to focus on liberty. As our concerns shift from survival to development, we gradually lose our capacity to take the position of those who are still preoccupied with survival. When we design structures for their survival, those structures prove progressively less suited to their needs. We have today reached a point where our designs kill not only the poor but ourselves. Consider, for example, urban renewal, begun in the late 1940's to house the poor in the city, now ceding the renewed city to renters and owners charged well beyond our capacity to pay, leaving many more of us homeless.

The struggle of the poor for survival has long since been outside of our experience. Only they can teach us their needs. Moreover, they can do that only as peers, with rights and duties complementary to and not subordinate to ours. To live together as peers, rather than as elites and masses, is new for us. We need guidelines to show us how to go about it. That, too, we will have to learn with the poor.

VIII

The Magnificat and the Economy

If sin, for the poor, is submission to an oppressive situation (Ex 32; Richard, p. 8; *Pacem in Terris,* #44), then virtue is action for liberation. If repentance, for the non-poor, is giving food and coats to the poor (Lk 3:10–11), then sin is accumulating these when others are cold and hungry.

In Scripture the primary characteristic distinguishing Yahweh from other gods, Richard concludes, is that "Yahweh's power is liberating" (p. 10). In our times "liberation from every oppressive situation" (Synod, p. 2) has become the hope of the world's poor; seeking ways of realizing this hope, their organizing task. A theology that mandates that liberating task transforms the church and defines the good news (De Santa Ana; Dorr; Gutiérrez; Herzog). But because all they could do for so long was to endure, it is difficult for the poor now to believe the good news, and harder still to find liberation among the central agenda of a church that, for many centuries, has given them consolation but not responsibility for a new exodus.

For the organizing poor, Marxism has been attractive for its promise of freedom from want. But most, if not all, Marxist states exhibit such restrictions on freedom that they are feared, both by those accustomed to democratic traditions and by those in totalitarian states who long for democratic institutions. Even in seeking economic and social security, unfreedom is too high a price to risk.

Another uniquely alienating aspect of Marxism is its atheism. It is not easy to struggle against principalities and powers not knowing where God is. Those organizing with the poor grow in the certainty that God is with them—witness Lisa Fitzgerald's testimony in the documentary from Nicaragua, *Report from the Front* (Skylark Productions, 1984). For the timid poor, various church documents carry a promise of liberation through action beyond earlier dreams (*Pacem in Terris, The Development of Peoples, Call to Action, On Human Work*). The poor were once taught that the promises embodied in these documents—the right to human development, the duty to seek effective political and economic alternatives, the promise of ownership through work—were merely secular, not sacred, initiatives. Now, in small communities, they are learning to claim their rights in reflecting on the Bible and with the support of liturgy and prayer (LADOC; Cardenal; Adriance; Berryman).

But people who are poor also have doubts. So many of the traditional symbols of their faith call for unquestioning trust in established authorities, so many sermons sunder the spiritual from the material, and so many organizations bent on material well-being disparage their religious commitment, it is hard for them to act without fear of worshiping idols (Richard). But some theologians understand and speak to their experience. Fashioning the elements of a liberation theology for Chicanos over a decade of study, teaching, and action, in 1986 Andres Guerrero presented a symbol of liberation from Chicano history and culture: Our Lady of Guadalupe. He is fully aware that this symbol has been used by church and state to keep Mexicans down; he is also aware that it embodies a dynamism that raises Mexicans up. The woman of Guadalupe appeared to a *mestizo*, a man without power, but a member of a group grounded in the dual cultural heritages of the dominated and the dominators and so privy to contradictory symbol systems. The good news learned from this situation, notes Guerrero, is that epitomized in the Magnificat—good news understood in the experience of the oppressed. Although songs and stories in different cultural settings have emphasized varying verses of Mary's song of praise, the ones the Chicano and Chicana hear today are the central lines:

God has put down the mighty from their thrones
and exalted those of low degree;
He has filled the hungry with good things
and the rich he has sent away empty (Lk 1:52–53).

These lines mean that God empowers the people and supports them in their liberation struggle; they also mean that the unwillingness to accept God's help in this liberating effort is sinful (Richard, p. 8). It is a long time since we have considered sin in this social context—in the context, that is, of a people's mandate to move out of bondage into a safe and productive city of God, sustained by God's ever-present help but responsible for its own destiny. Even today, many people with religious commitment divide over whether sin is personal or social.

When sin is only personal, the sinner seeks to make amends within the social order; but when the social order itself is perceived as sinful, virtue demands the reformation of that order. The threat of nuclear war, the destruction of poor people, racism, sexism, and the denial of human rights are social sins.

To articulate the right of the poor to share in the world's resources, Guerrero employed the concept of *La Raza Cósmica,* a concept used by Chicanos to label their peculiar experience of sharing equally in the culture of oppressor and oppressed, repudiating the evils of both and celebrating their strengths, symbolized in the Guadalupe story, in which a woman speaks to a man and urges the construction of a church to bridge the gap dividing oppressed and oppressor. But how is such a church built in modern society?

The Canadian church supports a society that is at once capitalist and socialist. The bishops in the United States cautiously explore the concepts of peace and of the economy. In the Magnificat, Mary states the resolution simply. If the mighty are brought down and those of low degree raised up, power is shared in some yet-to-be-tested way. When the hungry are filled with good things and the rich sent away empty, then the poor, fed, will no longer be poor, and the previously rich will have the same right to food.

Shared authority is an experiment in process. The poor, who experience the injustice of the present system, are summoned by God to change that system. For the rich and powerful, the summons is to let go.

IX

A Socio-Theology of Relinquishment

Seventeen years ago, "liberation theology" came to name theological reflection on the Latin American experience of finding God in the struggle for freedom, the struggle of peoples newly organized to claim their rights to the fruits of the earth, their rights to survive as peoples.

In biblical reflection on the oppressions they experienced, the poor discovered a mandate to claim the land and they reached out to take what was rightfully theirs. It is a right they found affirmed in the *Pastoral Constitution on the Church in the Modern World* (#69), where it is traced back, through St. Thomas Aquinas (II-II, Q.66, a.7) and the early "Fathers," to its roots in Leviticus (25:23). It is a right formalized in 1967 by the United Nations International Declaration of Human Rights:

1. All peoples have the right of self-determination. By virtue of that right they freely determine their political, social and cultural development.
2. All peoples may, for their own ends, freely dispose of their natural wealth and resources without prejudice to any obligations arising out of international economic co-operation, based upon the principle of mutual benefit, and international law. In no case may a people be deprived of its means of subsistence (United Nations, 1976, p. 4).

This theology, linking salvation to human liberation and land ownership to whole peoples, grew out of a suffering no longer necessary, in view of the world's resources, advances in technology, and the development of the world's peoples. The guarantee given in Leviticus 25 that people need not suffer the permanent loss of their land and the program outlined there for a just return of the land cry out for implementation, now that the conditions for its realization exist.

Problems which once required endurance and gave rise to distressing ethical choices regarding who should live and who should die now have a technical solution and demand ethical application of a well-defined doctrine of human rights. "Let my people go" is an ancient cry of the people. What is new—the change came about within a single generation, from 1960 to 1980—are the conditions for realizing it (Avila).

Theology is the search for God that rises out of human experience. For the Latin American poor, that experience was one of dispossession. Their formulation of a theology to reflect on their experience has prompted concerned people in northern hemisphere states to formulate a corresponding theology based on their own quite different experience. In North America, where some experience serious deprivation but the nation as a whole is materially affluent, theological reflection reveals a biblical summons to the non-poor which, while distinct from the call to the poor, is related to it and is grounded in the same gospel.

Recognizing that the labels "first," "second" and "third" worlds designate only a sequence of historical emergence and not priorities of right or status, it may be said that liberation theology is a third world phenomenon calling for first and second world responses. In North America, theology of liberation emerges as an answer to the question posed by third world peoples. When the poor reach out to take what is rightfully theirs, what response does the gospel require of those who are not poor?

The political response of North America to that question has been a show of resistance, based on the premise that national self-interest comes first in foreign affairs. Economically, our response has been to set production goals geared to individual needs on the assumption that world resources are scarce. Socially, we have joined a class struggle on the premise—spelled out in Wilson's sociobiology, for example—that the advantage of the powerful is a given of human nature. In view of what the signs of the times indicate as feasible today, the question of the poor deserves a sounder theological response, one rooted in biblical reflection and capable of fostering a new international will to guarantee freedom and life for the community of God's people.

When the social order exhibits an indifference to the survival of peoples, the religious search for God's will moves from the priestly celebration of life as it is being lived to the prophetic call for social reform (Weber). In response, then, to the question of what the gospel mandates of the non-poor, the tentative answer is: to release our grasp on the things the poor need to survive. The model is John the Baptist's formulation of his relationship with Jesus: "He must increase while I must decrease."

What is required at this time is not a theological initiative on the part of the first and second worlds but a response to an initiative already taken by developing peoples. In the course of first and second world development, developing peoples have been objects. Having heard the good news that the land belongs to the people, they are taking their place in history as subjects—no longer as slaves nor as dominators, not as followers of foreign leaders, even of those disposed to help the poor, but as partners in a common enterprise.

Although its remnants persist, especially in our attitudes toward work and workers, the history of servitude is closed. With regard to work, church doctrine has already been formulated; it only awaits application in teaching, learning and living (John Paul II; Baum). While the worker's rights have already been given theological formulation in the social encyclicals and their role as partners has been facilitated to some extent by the challenge to customs that have lost much of their efficacy as mechanisms of social control, that partnership is still impeded by outmoded class structures still informed by inadequate images of God.

In assembling the data that ground a theology of liberation for North America, three questions should be borne in mind: (1) How many people are there in your community? (2) What continent customarily predominated in maps of the world in your primary and secondary school social science classes? (3) What international encounter—North-South or East-West—provides the more salient context for politico-economic activity today?

Theological reflection is grounded in the signs of the times (Ratzinger). But which signs? From a sociological perspective, population shifts and trends are basic to all structural changes. The fact that the command of Genesis to "increase and multiply and fill the earth" is nearing fulfillment provides the basic context today of our understanding of human needs.

Ten thousand years ago, there were very few people on the earth. It took another 9,850 years for world population to reach a billion. Then, in just 100 years, the population more than doubled. From 2.5 billion in 1950, world population grew to four billion in 1975. It is projected to reach 6.2 billion by the year 2000 (Population Reference Bureau, World Population Growth Chart).[1]

First world peoples have responded to this population growth with fear—fear of hunger, of poverty, of pollution. In 1950, this fear was named: hanging over us was the threat of the population bomb. An academic response emerged in the "lifeboat" ethic, which argued persuasively that, for all practical purposes, we have to let the populations of poor nations die lest we all die (Hardin, 1974, 1979). And who are the peoples of the future, our progeny? The World Population Chart provides the answer. Between 1975 and 2000, only a replacement population is projected for Oceania, North America, Europe and the Soviet Union. But the populations of Africa, Asia and Latin America will double or nearly double.

From a Christian perspective, these are our progeny, but that is hardly the way they are perceived in practice. In the nations of Asia, Africa and Latin America, small wars are waged with weapons supplied by first and second world nations, in which arms production is an essential part of the economy. Asians and Latin Americans who emigrate to North American cities are seen by this country's poor as competitors for scarce jobs, housing and social security. In a frame of values that defines it as a priority task, producing resources for human need could challenge our imaginations. We are not dealing with a problem for which there is no technical solution. In many places, the development of goods and services for most of the population is a task scarcely touched by technology. The best estimate assures adequate resources (Murphy; George; World Resource Institute).

The pattern of decisions emanating from policymakers in affluent countries suggests that people in nations that have stable populations and for whom an abundant future appears threatened by third world development may secretly will the death of developing peoples. Witness the decisions to contain nuclear armament but to continue exporting conventional arms to nations waging small wars; to pay farmers not to produce food for nations too poor to buy it; to destroy designs for durable goods in a planned obsolescence program to stimulate the market in which affluent peoples buy and sell; to resolve balance of payment problems by usurping the raw materials of developing nations in exchange for products they do not need and which are not designed for their use (Baum and Cameron). These are the pragmatic rules of an economy that assumes scarcity, when, in fact, there are adequate resources and technology to further develop them and meet the needs of all (L. Brown, 1985; Bouvier, 1983; Murphy, 1983, 1984, 1985).

As a human community, we are capable of inventing what we think we need. One social function of religion is to set standards against which to measure ourselves as a human community. By summoning us to reform the unjust society, to celebrate the just society, and to save God's people from the evil and ignorance rooted in human choices (Bellah et al.), the religious perspective includes in the definition of needs the whole human community and challenges us to design the products and systems required to meet those needs.

Were the continents of the earth still one land mass (as they once were), with Africa at its center, it might be easier to think of the world as one land for one people. While all Christians, theoretically, think of the world of 5 billion persons as their community, that has hardly been true in practice. It might be utopian, moreover, to hope that it would be otherwise as long as a burgeoning threat of overpopulation kept our fears alive. It is only because the problem is now solvable that we can dare to address it, focusing our best human energies on it, motivated by God's will and guided by God's help.

Since about 1970, those who make population projections have become increasingly aware that world population is moving toward an upper limit, beyond which it will not go. Since 1980 we have been able to predict with increasing certainty that world population is likely to level off at around 10.5 billion, since population declines with the increase of per capita gross national product. There is nothing mystical about this link. It is just that, when our children stay alive, we plan to provide for them, and that planning creates the context for choices about family size. Poverty level is the critical element in the choice about family size (see Murphy, 1983, 1984, 1985).

Poverty is defined operationally here as high infant mortality and low life-expectancy due to lack of food, clothing and shelter. A careful observation of population by country confirms that population size tends to diminish with the decline in poverty, although the rate of decline is slower for countries with low technological development. At the same time, ever more accurate computer calculations of world resources indicate that the carrying capacity of the world's natural resources—most of which are renewable and which can be extended by scientific methods of production, conversion and reclamation—has an upper limit of about 35 billion people, far more than we will ever have to provide for.[2]

Although this information is now common knowledge (Bouvier; Murphy; Brown, 1985), it must nevertheless be used with caution, for the simple reason that the fact that something can be done does not mean that it will be done. The knowledge that feeding, clothing and sheltering the whole human population are problems with a technical solution is good news for the poor. The bad news is that world resources will not be used to keep the poor alive unless those with prior access to these resources give up their hold on them. History reveals that, when people are able to supply their basic needs, they tend to generate more and more needs within the limit set by their values. It is this reality that demands new theological reflection and formulation.

Anthropologist Clifford Geertz notes that each religion, as a cultural system, contains "a unique and surprising message." Christianity's message—sometimes wonderfully drawing people beyond established selfishness, sometimes scandalously coopted by the established pattern—is its preference for the poor and its witness to human altruism.

Sociologists recognize that the message of religion, looked at as a social institution, is frequently used by the political economy's powerful role-players as a means to get others to do their bidding (Dawson). In the last analysis, power comes down to control over violence; short of that, it includes control over land, labor, industry, trade and the unknown (B. Moore). It is not the essential function of religion to be used as a tool in struggles for control, but that has been one of the hazards it has historically encountered.

At its core, the Christian story is of God-become-incarnate and dying for a sinful people. The good news is that an act of disinterested love, made possible by a grace that is abundant, transforms and saves (Mt 10:17–27). The implication is that human behavior is not necessarily selfish; with grace building on nature, human beings may rise to a disinterested love of the other. That is what Christian love is about.

Religion has been used to channel the energies of people in a particular nation to act in their own-self-interest. That has been explored as idolatry. When religion is called on now to offer guidelines for a global community, its use to justify the self-interested choices of a particular nation is more easily recognized as idolatry. What is needed today is a theology for North America that is part of a larger theology for the world, a North American response to an initiative taken by our Latin American colleagues (Gutiérrez; Sobrino; Richard), whose insights are in turn rooted in the struggles of the world's conscientized poor (Freire). The one gospel, which Latin American liberation theology brings to bear on the just demands of the organizing poor as they reach out to take what is rightfully theirs, expects of us an answer.

Some popular religious expressions in this country, however, seem to be, not an answer to the cries of the poor, but rather a hardening of hearts against them. Witness some of the preaching of the new religious right which is heard and seen in the electronic church and which celebrates capitalism, affirms the arms race, justifies racism and keeps women subservient, claiming to give life but all the time undermining the will to respond to the organizing poor.

Religions, with their surprising messages, are both prophetic—denouncing evil in society—and priestly—reinforcing in worship, prayer, song, dance and art the good that people strive to do. Because it calls one to account, prophecy hurts. Before we offer our gifts, prophecy makes us go out to right a wrong, leaving our gifts at the altar (Mt 5:23–24). This disturbs the even tenor of our lives, forces us to raise to consciousness daily choices of which we are often not aware, upsets an equilibrium resting on class advantage. It is easier to kill or at least discredit the prophets: then one can go on as usual. That is why powerful people seek to control education, media and religion.

If others, using the regular channels of communication, define the situation for us, we scarcely become aware of the contradiction between the surprising message of our preferred religious tradition and the actual witness of our lives and of the political economy in which we live. We use symbols to reflect on life's challenges; but if we are unable to name an evil, we are powerless to consider its consequences.

Religions are not private matters; they bind together or fragment a people. That is why, when there were multiple tribes, there were multiple gods. For the one human community there is one God; but the tribes are still caught up in a struggle—idolatrous, in theological perspective—to co-opt the one God (Richard; Marstin).

Many of the elements of a North American theology are already in place. The option for the poor was clearly reiterated at the Second Vatican Council (Dorr; Ratzinger) and a theology of

work, developed in the anniversary social encyclicals, is concluded in the 90th-year letter, *Laborem Exercens,* promulgated by
Pope John Paul II in 1981. Canadians have done much more with
this document than we have in the U.S., but the content is richly
articulated in our workshops and publications (Baum; O'Brien
and Shannon; Walsh and Davies; Coston).[3]

In 1891, Pope Leo XIII's *Rerum Novarum* ("On the Conditions
of the Working Class") appeared as the Church's first major response to the nineteenth century challenge to free itself from its
entanglement in an increasingly unjust social order. The Pope
said that, of the profits of industry, workers have a right to a just
share—enough to live with their families in simple dignity. Pope
Pius XI recalled that right in 1931, in his *Quadragesimo Anno,* and
added the directive that workers have a right to organize in labor
unions and to use the strike and boycott to demand of industry
their claim to a fair share of the profit. The document's English
title, "On the Reconstruction of the Social Order," serves as a
reminder that the problem being addressed is institutionalized in
social structures that need to be changed. In 1961, Pope John
XXIII promulgated *Mater et Magistra* ("Christianity and Social
Progress") in which he called to account the church in Latin
America for being aligned too closely with established centers of
power and wealth and directed it to set out a justice agenda
based on the cries of the poor.

In 1971, Pope Paul VI added *Octogesima Adveniens,* remind-
ing us that it was the 80th anniversary of *Rerum Novarum* and calling us to political action. The English title, "A Call to Action,"
expressed well the message of the encyclical which was that,
with the emergence of multinational corporations that are not
under the control of any sovereign state, we must take political
action to bring social institutions into line with principles of social
justice. In *Laborem Exercens,* published in 1981, Pope John Paul II
proclaimed the priority of labor over capital in the endeavor by
those who work the land and develop the technology to produce
the things we need for survival (Baum; Baum and Cameron).

Between 1960 and 1970, in the elaboration of its theological
position on human development and church ministry, the
church shifted the primary focus of ministry from alleviating the

results of poverty—the long-standing goal of human service—to eliminating its causes—a shift recognizable in its post-Vatican II position, the reasons for which were spelled out by the Canadian bishops in 1971.

In formulating the role of the church in the world, *Mater et Magistra* marked a turning point. It called to account the Latin American church because that continent which was over ninety percent Catholic, was a witness to the world of the effect of the church's presence in society. As at the time of the French Revolution, the entrenchment and co-optation of the institutional church—which counseled the poor to wait for heaven, although they were enduring unnecessary and unjust suffering, while their elite neighbors enjoyed an affluent life—witnessed to oppression.

Just as, two hundred years earlier, urban workers in Europe were moving out of servitude even as the church participated in the servitude of the still-suffering farm workers, African nations in 1960 were moving out of colonial servitude, with some missionaries participating in their struggle but others tolerating established injustices. *Mater et Magistra* was a warning to church workers, who were allied with established wealth and power even as their ministry was alive with the good news of liberation, not to let the old bias reassert itself (Adriance).

In the United States at the same time—that is, in 1960—the struggle of Catholic European immigrants was coming to an end and Christian families with newly-won affluence were being called to account for their indifference to and even participation in racism in the inner city and the rural south (Pettigrew and Campbell). Long programmed to assist the ethnics in the tasks of citizenship, the church was now asked to take up the new agenda of Asian, African and Latin American oppression. Response to the new mission proved exciting in some quarters, sluggish in others.

In 1963, Pope John XXIII's *Pacem in Terris* proclaimed peace, poverty and human rights as the central concerns of committed Christians. The convocation of Vatican II was announced as a means of focusing the church's missionary zeal on the task of third world liberation. No institution was more directly affected

by this announcement than were the religious orders and congregations of men and women, which were instructed to renew
their structures for the purpose of effectively implementing the
council directives. Obedience to their vows took on new meaning; the religious communities' response constitutes a saga in its
own right (Neal, 1984).

Pope Paul VI's *Populorum Progressio*, issued in 1967, called
the development of peoples, on the basis of universal human
rights, the church's mission. That mission was reaffirmed in the
Call to Action of 1971, and that year's Synod of Bishops gave
guidelines for its implementation in *Justice in the World*. Every diocese, religious congregation and teaching center was instructed
to establish justice commissions. Action in behalf of justice was
proclaimed a constitutive dimension of the preaching of the gospel. And, lest anyone should miss its meaning, the Synod spoke
of "the church's mission for the redemption of the human race
and its liberation from every oppressive situation" (#6).

The documents reactivated the promise of Leviticus 25 and
explained Luke 3 in modern terms, pointing out how sin should
be understood if repentance means giving to the poor our second
coat and our abundant food. They reminded us that the rich
young man turned aside from the mission not because he was
not virtuous but because he found it too hard to give up control
of wealth and power (Mt 10).

Small wonder that a new excitement stirred the third world.
But for North American Catholics, long accustomed to struggling
against adversity as members of an immigrant church, we were
hesitant about taking on the agenda of the non-poor. We could
not feel any excitement about letting go our hold on a status so
recently won. Jesus' promise in Matthew 6 to care for us as he
did the flowers of the field did not inspire our trust. We had
worked too hard for what we had acquired to believe that we
would still have sufficient if we let others share in it. We had such
a crisis of faith we dared lose sight of God's presence among the
poor as they reached out to claim what was rightfully theirs. We
accused them of atheism, thus justifying our greed. We are still
ambivalent about sharing the resources of the earth, still willing
to use violence, and still easily influenced by ideological ma-

nipulation of symbols by the media. That is why theology is needed.

How do we make an ethic of altruism a vital part of our corporate witness? How does an option for the poor become an effective program to eliminate the known causes of poverty? How do we turn a utopian ideal into a technical solution? These are the tasks of a pedagogy inspired by a theology of relinquishment, a theology for letting go our grasp on the things the poor need for their development.

If the aspirations of the disinherited for liberation from political, cultural, economic and social oppression are the major signs of our times (Ratzinger, p. 195), then our preferential option for the poor will focus on human rights. We are only beginning to be aware of the relevance for theology of the United Nations' International Bill of Human Rights. In no prior historical era have equal recognition and status been accorded to all human beings. Even as it has prompted us toward affirmations of justice and freedom with ever wider applicability, the church has managed historically to tolerate what society at large has tolerated, from slavery to serfdom to worker exploitation.

Society is today invited to proclaim the basic rights of all human beings not only to political freedoms—a strong American tradition—but to the resources of health, education and welfare that provide social, cultural and economic security—a socialist idea (Cassidy). These latter rights we in the United States still treat as a privilege for those with wages for their work—a conception that allows us, on the one hand, to neglect needed work because we cannot see how it could be funded and, on the other, to ignore the health, education and welfare of people without jobs.

The understaffing of human services and the deterioration of public property cry out for more workers. Inadequate funding prevents a solution, however, and our imaginations are fettered by institutional restraints (United Nations, 1980, p. 45). Capitalist and communist ideologies differ on the question of how to implement rights to political freedom and economic security, and the conflict between them blocks the solution to many human problems. It is not a technical problem but a social, political and economic one, one that calls for religious motivation to free our narrowed vision from cultural constraints that are outdated in view of our human resources and technological potential.

Unaligned nations welcome assistance from capitalist and communist nations alike because they do not give priority to one set of rights over the other. Neither political freedom nor economic security is adequate by itself for a fully human life; people need both. If these human rights are to be incorporated into public economic and social contracts, the enlightened self-interest which now dominates our social analysis must be replaced by the institutionalization of altruism as public virtue. One way to ground the effort needed to realize that task is through a developed theology of world community.

Such a theology would require several elements:

1. An affirmation of participatory decision-making as the dominant method of formulating public policy, founded on a relationship among members of all adult working groups that is circular rather than pyramidal. This principle is grounded in a recognition that peoples have a human right to participate as peers in the decisions that affect their lives. It also reflects the fact that, given our very different human experiences, we are all learners as well as teachers when it comes to world affairs.

2. An assumption of altruism as the basis of public virtue instead of self-interest as natural virtue. The privatization of religion should be recognized as an ideological ploy.

3. A pedagogy for teaching and learning about God that includes action for righting social wrongs as well as reflection on human experience.

4. Deliberation on a new international economic order, since the present economic order, for all its potential natural and human resources, falls far short of providing for human needs.

5. A shift of emphasis from who God is to where God is in considering the immediate future. While we cannot know God

fully in any historical era, we can discover manifestations of God's presence in reading the signs of the times.

Existing pyramidal structures—in which decision-making is the prerogative of men but not women, or the first world but not the third world, or West but not East, or North but not South—are inadequate for resolving world problems. Decisions are based on too narrow an experience by managers who are not accountable to all those who are affected by their decisions and who are, after all, their peers. The results are to be seen in the arms race, in world hunger and poverty, in environmental destruction, in conflicts among ethnic groups, in the instability of family life, and in media manipulation of symbol and truth. Only a tradition of shared decision-making holds the promise of solving the problems of human need.

The assumption that powerful nations, with their control over the use of violence, can legitimately shape world decisions in their own interest no longer deserves the support of the churches. Its illegitimacy is amply demonstrated by its cost in human life. An institutionalization of altruism is needed to protect human rights to both political freedom and economic security; alternative structures of political economy need to be created to that end, and a theology is needed to legitimate the effort. One place to begin is in the Catholic university, where a circular model of teaching and learning will itself point the way toward a circular model of decision-making.

Every age invites new understanding of God. Ours suggests that God is uniquely with the poor as they reach out to take what is rightfully theirs. As one recent religious formulation of that insight puts it: "Inherent in our developing understanding of mission is the belief that God, who speaks to us through diverse ways, today calls to us with special insistence through the voices of the materially poor as they attempt to organize themselves to claim their rights as human beings" (Sisters' Survey, 1980, Item 395). God has long been sought in the quiet of the mountaintop. Now we are invited to greet the living God in the city and the countryside in the struggle for and the sharing of the bread.

Appendix

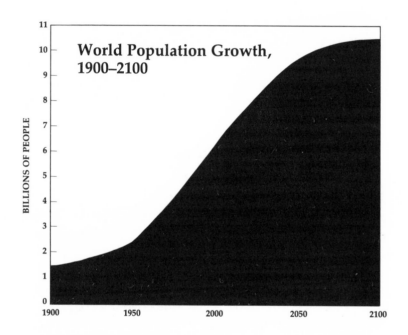

World Population Growth, 1900–2100

BILLIONS OF PEOPLE

11
10
9
8
7
6
5
4
3
2
1
0

1900   1950   2000   2050   2100

Population Reference Bureau, 1984

World Population Growth

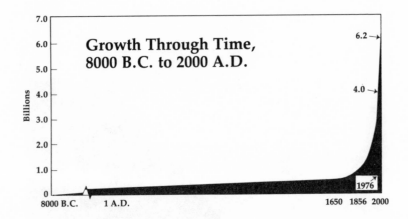

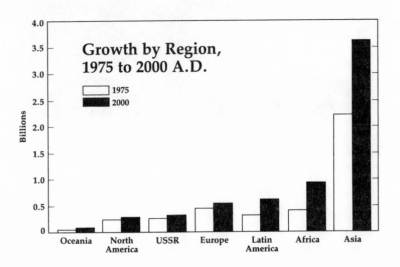

Bibliography

Abbott, Walter. M., S.J., ed. *The Documents of Vatican II*. New York: Guild Press, 1966.

A.D. 1977: reprint of the recommendations of the Detroit Call to Action meeting of Oct. 20–23, 1976, sponsored by the United States Catholic Conference of Bishops, Washington, D.C. Quixote Center, 1977.

Adriance, Madeleine Cousineau. *Option for the Poor: Brazilian Catholicism in Transition,* Sheed and Ward (1986).

Albrecht, Stan L. et al. *Social Psychology.* Englewood Cliffs, New Jersey: Prentice-Hall, 1980.

Allport, Gordon, *The Nature of Prejudice.* New York: Doubleday, 1958.

Allport, Gordon, "The Historical Background of Modern Social Psychology" in *The Handbook of Social Psychology,* second edition, edited by Gardner Lindzey and Elliot Aronson. Reading, Massachusetts: Addison-Wesley, Vol. I, 1968, pp. 1–80.

Allport, Gordon, "The Religious Context of Prejudice," *Journal of the Scientific Study of Religion,* Vol. 5, 1965, pp. 447–457.

Alves, Ruben, *A Theology of Human Hope.* New York: Corpus Books, 1969.

Appalachian Bishops' Pastoral, "This Land Is Home to Me." in O'Brien and Shannon, pp. 468–516.

Appiah-Kubi, Kofi and Sergio Torres (eds.), *African Theology Route.* Papers from the Pan-African Conference of Third World Theologians, Accra, Ghana, 1977. Maryknoll, New York: Orbis, 1979.

Aquinas, Thomas, *Summa Theologica*. Three volumes. Trans. by the Fathers of the English Dominican Province. New York: Benziger Bros., 1947.

Arroyo, C., S.J. "Justice for Latin America," *LADOC*, Vol. 11, p. 16. Washington D.C.: United States Catholic Conference, 1972.

Avila, Charles, *Ownership*. Maryknoll, New York: Orbis, 1983.

Avila, Rafael, *Worship and Politics*. Maryknoll, New York: Orbis, 1981.

Bainbridge, William Sims and Rodney Stark. "Consciousness Reformation Reconsidered," *Journal for the Scientific Study of Religion*, Vol. 20, No. 1, 1981, pp. 1–16.

Banks, Walter R., "Two Impossible Revolutions? Black Power and Church Power," *Journal for the Scientific Study of Religion*, Vol. 8, pp. 263–268.

Baran, P. *The Political Economy of Growth*. New York: Modern Reader, 1968.

Barash, David P. *Sociobiology and Behavior*. New York: Elsevier, 1977.

Barnet, Richard J., and Ronald E. Muller, *Global Reach*. New York: Simon & Schuster, 1974.

Barraclough, Geoffrey, "Wealth and Power: The Politics of Food and Oil," *New York Review of Books*, August 7, 1975.

Baum, Gregory, "The Christian Left at Detroit," *The Ecumenist*, Sept.–Oct., 1975, reprinted in *Theology in the Americas*, ed. by Sergio Torres and John Eagleson. Maryknoll, New York: Orbis Books, 1976.

Baum, Gregory, *Catholics and Canadian Socialism: Political Thought in the Thirties and the Forties*. Toronto: Lorimer, 1980.

Baum, Gregory, *The Priority of Labor*. New York: Paulist Press, 1982.

Baum, Gregory, and Duncan Cameron, *Ethics and Economics: Canada's Catholic Bishops and the Economic Crisis*. Toronto: James Larimer and Co., 1984.

Baumann, Donald J., R.B. Cialdini, D.T. Kenrick. "Altruism as Hedonism: Helping and Self Gratification as Equivalent Responses," *Journal of Personality and Social Psychology*, Vol. 40, No. 6, June 1981, pp. 1039–1046.

Bellah, Robert N., *Beyond Belief: Essays on Religion in a Post-Traditional World*. New York: Harper and Row, 1970.

Bellah, Robert N., *The Broken Covenant: American Civil Religion in Time of Trial*. New York: Seabury, 1975.

Bellah, Robert N., *Habits of the Heart: Individualism and Commitment in American Life*, Berkeley: University of California Press, 1985.

Bellah, Robert N. and Phillip E. Hammond, *Varieties of Civil Religion*. San Francisco: Harper and Row, 1980.

Berger, Peter L., *The Sacred Canopy*. New York: Doubleday Anchor Books, 1969.

Berger, Peter L., *Pyramids of Sacrifice: Political Ethics and Social Change*. New York: Basic Books, 1974.

Berger, Peter L. and Thomas Luckmann, *The Social Construction Reality: A Treatise on the Sociology of Knowledge*. New York: Doubleday, 1967.

Bernadin, J., "Colonnese's Dismissal," IDOC 34: 30–31, New York, 1971.

Berryman, Phillip, *The Religious Roots of Rebellion: Christians in Central American Revolutions*. Maryknoll, New York: Orbis Books, 1984.

Blanchette, Claudia Ann, "Social Justice: Mandate and Dilemma for Roman Catholic Religious Education in the Light of the Second Vatican Council," Dissertation submitted to Boston University, 1979. Unpublished.

Bliss, Shepard, "Jimmy Carter: Trilateralism in Action," *Guardian*, Feb. 16, 1977, p. 15.

Blumer, H., *Symbolic Interaction: Perspective and Method*. Englewood Cliffs: Prentice-Hall, Inc., 1969.

Bouvier, Leon F., "Planet Earth 1984–2034: A Demographic Vision." *Population Bulletin*, Vol. 39, No. 1, Feb. 1984, Population Reference Bureau, 2213 M Street, Washington, D.C., 20037.

Brazilian Bishops' 1976 *Pastoral Letter: This Land Is Home to Me*, (translated from the Portuguese of *Jornal O Estado de S. aulo*, Terga-Ferra, 16 de Nov. de 1976, p. 1).

Brown, Lester R., ed. *State of the World: 1985*. New York: W.W. Norton, 1985.

Brown, Robert McAfee, *Theology in a New Key: Responding to Liberation Themes*. Philadelphia: Westminster Press, 1978.

Burger, Thomas, "Talcott Parsons: The Problems of Order in Society and the Program of an Analytical Sociology," *American Journal of Sociology*, Summer 1983.

Cabestrero, Teofilo, *Ministers of God: Ministers of the People*. Maryknoll, New York: Orbis Books, 1983.

Cabral, Amilcar, "The Weapon of Theory," in *Revolution in Guinea*. Ed. and trans. Richard Handyside. New York: Monthly Review Press, 1969, pp. 90–111.

Call to Action, the Justice Conference Resolutions, *Origins*, NC Documentary Service, Vol. 6, Nos. 20 and 21, Nov. 4 and 11, 1976, pp. 311–340.

Callahan, William, *Quest for Justice*. The Center of Concern, 3700 13th Street, N.E. Washington, D.C. 20017, 1972.

Camara, Dom H., *Spiral of Violence*. Denville, New Jersey: Dimension Books, 1971.

Campbell, D., "Ethnocentrism and Other Altruistic Motives." In D. Levine (ed.) Nebraska Symposium on Motivation. Lincoln: University of Nebraska Press. 1965, pp. 283–311.

Campbell, D., "On the Genetics of Altruism and the Counterhedonic Components in Human Culture." In Wispe, pp. 39–55.

Canadian Conference of Bishops, "Towards a Coalition for Development." Strategy Committee Report, 1969, p. 8.

Caplan, Arthur L., *The Sociobiology Debate: Readings in Ethical and Scientific Issues*. New York: Harper and Row, 1978.

Cardenal, Ernesto, *The Gospel in Solentiname*. Maryknoll, New York: Orbis Books, 1976.

Cassidy, Richard, *Catholic Teaching Regarding Capitalism and Socialism*. Detroit: Office of Justice and Peace, Archdiocese of Detroit, 1979.

Cerni, D.M., *Standards in Process: Foundations and Profiles of ISDN and OSI Studies*. U.S. Department of Commerce: National Telecommunications and Information Administration, 1984.

Chomsky, Noam, "Intervention in Vietnam and Central America," *Monthly Review*, September 1985.

Christ, Carol and Judith Plaskow, *Womanspirit Rising*. New York: Harper and Row, 1979.

Cole, E., *House of Bondage*. New York: Random House, 1971.

Coleman, John, in *Theology in the Americas*, ed. by Sergio Torres and John Eagleson. Maryknoll, New York: Orbis Books, 1976, pp. 379–387.

Collins, Randall and Michael Makowsky, *The Discovery of Society*. New York: Random House, 1984.

Colonnese, L.M., *Conscientization for Liberation*. Washington, D.C.: Division for Latin America, United States Catholic Conference, 1971.

Comblin, Jose, Notes on a Meeting: "Growth of Fraternal Communities." Diocese of Crateus, Brazil. Translated by Loretta Slover, 1971.

Comblin, Jose, *The Meaning of Mission*. Tr. by John Drury. Maryknoll, New York: 1977.

Comblin, Jose, "The Bishops' Conference at Puebla," *Theology Digest*, Vol. 23, No. 1, Spring 1980, pp. 9–12.

Comte, August, *The Positive Philosophy of August Comte*. New York: Calvin Blanchard, 1858.

Cone, James H., *God of the Oppressed*, New York: Seabury Press, 1975.

Conway, Jim, *Marx and Jesus*. New York: Carlton Press, 1973.

Cotter, J.T., "Christians for Socialism Conference Voices Controversial Challenge," *Latin America Calls*, Vol. 9, (1972), No. 5: 4–5.

Cussianovich, Alejandro, S.D.B., *Religious Life and the Poor: Liberation Theology Perspectives*. Maryknoll, New York: Orbis, 1979.

Daly, Mary, *Beyond God the Father*. Boston: Beacon Press, 1973.

Daly, Mary, *Gyn Ecology: The Medical Ethics of Radical Feminism*. Boston: Beacon Press, 1978.

Dawkins, Richard, *The Selfish Gene*. New York: Oxford University Press, 1976.

Dawson, Christopher, *Religion and Culture*. New York: Sheed and Ward, 1948.

Desmond, C., *The Discarded People*. Baltimore: Penguin Books, Inc., 1971.

de Castro, Josue de, *Death in the Northeast.* New York: Random House, 1969.

De Santa Ana, Julio, *Toward a Church of the Poor.* Maryknoll, New York: Orbis, 1979.

Devore, Irven and Scot Morris. "The New Science of Genetic Self-Interest," *Psychology Today*, February, 1977, pp. 42–51, 84–88.

Dodd, C.H., *The Parables of the Kingdom.* New York: Scribner Publishers, 1961.

"Dom Helder Camara Denounces." Brazilian Information Service. May 1972: No. 7, p.3.

Dorr, Donal, *Option for the Poor: A Hundred Years of Vatican Social Teaching.* Maryknoll, New York: Orbis Books, 1983.

Drinan, Robert J., S.J., "Kissinger Commission Puts U.S. on Wrong Side," *National Catholic Reporter*, April 27, 1984.

Durkheim, Emile, *Elementary Forms of the Religious Life.* New York: Collier Books, 1961.

Eagleson, John, ed., *Christians and Socialism.* Maryknoll, New York: Orbis, 1975.

Eagleson, John and Philip Scharper (eds.), *Puebla and Beyond.* Maryknoll, New York: Orbis, 1979.

Eliade, Mircea, *From Primitives to Zen.* New York: Harper and Row, 1967.

Erdozain, Placido, *Archbishop Romero: Martyr of Salvador.* Maryknoll, New York: Orbis, 1981.

Evans, Robert A. and Alice F. Evans. *Human Rights: A Dialogue between the First and Third World.* Maryknoll, New York: Orbis Books, 1983.

Fanon, Frantz, *Black Skins, White Masks.* New York: Grove Press, 1968 (originally published, 1952).

Fanon, Frantz, *Wretched of the Earth.* New York: Grove Press, 1968.

Fenn, Richard K. *Toward a Theory of Secularization.* Society for the Scientific Study of Religion, Monograph Series, No. 1, 1978.

Ferree, William, *The Act of Social Justice.* Dayton, Ohio: Marianist Publications, 1951.

Fiorenza, Elisabeth Schüssler, *In Memory of Her: A Feminist Theo-*

ological Reconstruction of Christian Origins. New York: Cross-road, 1983.

Flannery, Austin, ed., *Vatican Council II: The Concilar and Post-Concilar Documents.* Northport, New York: Costello Publishing Co., 1975.

Freire, Paulo, "Conscientizing as a Way of Liberating," *LADOC* (A Documentation Service of the Division for Latin America). Washington, D.C.: United States Catholic Conference, 1972.

Freire, Paulo, *Pedagogy of the Oppressed.* New York: Herder and Herder, 1970.

Freire, Paulo, *The Politics of Education: Culture, Power and Liberation.* Massachusetts: Bergin and Garvey, 1985.

Freud, Sigmund, *The Future of an Illusion.* New York: Liveright Publishing Corp., 1949.

Fustel de Coulanges, N.D., *The Ancient City.* New York: Doubleday, 1963.

Gallup, George, *Forecast 2000.* New York: William Morrow, 1984.

Gardner, Anne Marie, ed., *Women and Catholic Priesthood: An Expanded Vision.* Proceedings of the Detroit Ordination Conference. New York: Paulist Press, 1976.

Garrett, William R., "Politicized Clergy: A Sociological Interpretation of the New Breed," *Journal for the Scientific Study of Religion,* Vol. 12, 1973, pp. 385–400.

Geertz, Clifford, "Religion as a Cultural System." In *Anthropological Approaches to the Study of Religion,* ed. Michael Banton. London: Tavistock, 1966.

Gehrig, Gail, "The American Civil Religion Debate: A Source for Theory Construction," *Journal for the Scientific Study of Religion,* Vol. 20, 1980, pp. 51–63.

Gehrig, Gail, *American Civil Religion: An Assessment.* Society for the Scientific Study of Religion, Monograph Series, no. 3, 1981.

George, Susan, *Ill Fares the Land: Essays on Food, Hunger and Power.* Washington D.C., Institute for Policy Studies, 1984.

GIST, "Human Rights," Bureau of Public Affairs, Department of State, September 1984.

Glock, Charles Y., "Images of 'God,' Images of Man, and the Organization of Social Life," *Journal for the Scientific Study of Religion*, Vol. 11, 1971, pp. 1–15.

Glock, Charles and Rodney Stark, *Christian Belief and Anti-Semitism*. New York: Harper and Row, 1966.

Glock, C.Y., B. Ringer and E.R. Babbie, *To Comfort and To Challenge*. Berkeley: University of California Press, 1967.

Gottwald, Norman K., ed. *The Bible and Liberation: Political and Social Hermeneutics*. Maryknoll, New York: Orbis, 1983.

Goulet, D. and M. Hudson, *The Myth of Aid*. New York: IDOC/North America, 432 Park Ave. South, New York, N.Y. 10016, 1973.

Greeley, Andrew M., *The Denominational Society*. Glenview, Illinois: Scott, Foresman and Company, 1972.

Greeley, Andrew M., *Priests in the United States*. New York: Doubleday and Co., Inc., 1972.

Greeley, Andrew M., *The Communal Catholic*. New York: Seabury Press, 1976.

Gregory, Michael S. et al. *Sociobiology and Human Nature*. San Francisco, California: Jossey-Bass, 1978.

Guerrero, Andres Gonzalez, *A Chicano Theology: Guadalupe and La Raza as Keys to Liberation*. Maryknoll, New York: Orbis, 1986.

Gutierrez, Gustavo M., "Notes for a Theology of Liberation." *Theological Studies*, Vol. 31, 1970, pp. 243–261.

Gutierrez, Gustavo M., *A Theology of Liberation*. Maryknoll, New York: Orbis, 1971.

Gutierrez, Gustavo M., *The Power of the Poor in History*. Maryknoll, New York: Orbis, 1983.

Hadden, Jeffrey K., "An Analysis of Some Factors Associated with Religion and Political Affiliation," *Journal for the Scientific Study of Religion*, Vol. 2, 1962, pp. 209–216.

Hammond, Phillip E. *The Sacred in a Post-Secular Age*. Berkeley, California: University of California Press, 1985.

Hanks, Thomas D., *God So Loved the Third World*. Maryknoll, New York: Orbis, 1983.

Hardin, Garrett, "The Tragedy of the Commons," *Science*, December 13, 1968, pp. 1243–1248.

Hardin, Garrett, *The Limits of Altruism*. Bloomington, Indiana: Indiana University Press, 1978.

Hardin, Garrett, "Living on a Lifeboat," *1974 Bioscience*, Vol. 24, No. 10, October 1974, pp. 561–568.

Hardin, Garrett, "The Survival of Nations and Civilizations," *Science*, Vol. 172, June 1971, p. 290.

Hegel, G.W.F., *Reason in History*. New York: Bobbs-Merrill, 1953.

Herzog, Frederick, *Justice Church: The New Function of the Church in North American Christianity*. Maryknoll, New York: Orbis Books, 1980.

Hinton, William, *Fanshen*. New York: Random House (Vintage), 1968.

Hofstadter, Richard, *Social Darwinism in American Thought*. Boston: Beacon Press, 1955.

Holland, Joe, *The American Journey: A Theology in the Americas*. IDOC/North America, in cooperation with the Center for Concern, Washington, D.C., 1976.

Holland, Joe and Peter Henriot, S.J., *Social Analysis: Linking Faith and Justice*. Maryknoll, New York: Orbis, rev. ed. 1983.

Houtart, F., "The Church and Development," *LADOC:* II, 17a. Washington, D.C.: United States Catholic Conference, 1969.

Huntington, Samuel, *Crisis of Democracy*. New York: New York University Press, 1975.

"I Accuse—An Indictment," CICOP Background Paper #4. Washington, D.C.: United States Catholic Conference, 1971.

INTERCOM: The International Population News Magazine. Population Reference Bureau, April 1980, Vol. 8, No. 4.

International Study Days, *For a Society Overcoming Domination*. Vol. 1: Deposit. New York: Valley Offset, 1978.

Jackson, George, *Soledad Brother*. New York: Bantam Books, 1970.

Jerome Biblical Commentary. Englewood Cliffs, N.J.: Prentice-Hall, 1968. "Prophecy," 223–237; "Beatitudes," 62–114.

John, Brother, O.S.B., "Tell Your People: The Plea of a Guatemalan Refugee Family," Weston Priory, March 2, 1983. Pamphlet.

John XXIII, *Mater et Magistra (Christianity and Social Progress)*. New York: America Press, 1961.

John XXIII, *Pacem in Terris*. Boston: St. Paul Editions, 1963.

John Paul II, *Laborem Exercens (On Human Work)*. Boston: St. Paul Editions, 1981.

Kolb, William L., "Images of Man and the Sociology of Religion," *Journal for the Scientific Study of Religion*, Vol. 1, 1961 pp. 5–29.

Kolko, G. and J., *The Limits of Power: World and United States Foreign Policy, 1945–1954*. New York: Harper and Row, 1972.

Kolko, G., *The Roots of American Foreign Policy*. Boston: Beacon Press, 1969.

Kolko, G., *The Triumph of Conservatism*. Chicago: Quadrangle Books, 1963.

Kopkind, Andrew "The Age of Reaganism," *The Nation*, November 3, 1984, pp. 448–451.

Küng, Hans, "Jesus' Challenge to the Church." Address delivered at the Paulist Center, Boston, November 13, 1972.

LADOC, *Basic Christian Communities*. Latin American Documentation, United States Catholic Conference, Washington, D.C., 1976.

Laing, R.D., *The Politics of the Family*. New York: Random House, 1969.

Lappe, Frances and Joseph Collins, *Food First: Beyond the Myth of Scarcity*, Boston: Houghton-Mifflin, 1977.

Latin America Calls. Washington, D.C.: Latin America Bureau, United States Catholic Conference, 1972.

Lenski, Gerhard, *The Religious Factor: A Sociological Study of Religion's Impact on Politics Economics and Family Life*. New York: Doubleday, 1963.

Leo XIII, *The Condition of Labor (Rerum Novarum*, 1891). Washington, D.C.: National Catholic Welfare Conference, 1942.

Lernoux, Penny, *Cry of the People*. New York: Simon and Schuster, 1980.

Lewontin, R.C., Steven Rose and Leon J. Camin, *Not in Our Genes*. New York: Pantheon Books, 1984.

Libano, J.B. "Experiences with the Base Christian Communities in Brazil." LADOC, Peru: Latinamerica Press, 1981.

Lodge, George C., *The New American Ideology*. New York: Alfred Knopf, 1975.

Maduro, Otto, *Religion and Social Conflicts*. Maryknoll, New York: Orbis, 1982.

Magdoff, H., *The Age of Imperialism*. New York: Monthly Review Press, 1969.

Mannheim, Karl, *Ideology and Utopia*. New York: Harcourt, Brace and World, Inc., 1936.

Marstin, Ronald, *Beyond Our Tribal Gods: The Maturing of Faith*. Maryknoll, New York: Orbis Books, 1979.

Martin, James, *The Telematic Society: A Challenge for Tomorrow*. Englewood Cliffs, N.J.: Prentice-Hall, 1981.

Marx, Karl and Friedrich Engels, Excerpts from "The German Ideology," in Lewis S. Feuer (ed.) *Basic Writings on Politics and Philosophy*. New York: Anchor Books, 1959.

May, M.A. and L.W. Doob, "Competition and Cooperation," New York: Social Science Research Council, *Bulletin*, No. 25, 1937.

Mbeke, Govan, *The Peasant Revolt*. Baltimore: Penguin Books, 1964.

McCullough, L. et al., "World Justice and Peace: A Radical Analysis for American Christians," 1972. Published by Project Four, Maryknoll, 110 Charles Street, Hingham, Mass. 02043.

McGinniss, James B., *Bread and Justice: Toward a New International Economic Order*. New York: Paulist Press, 1979.

McKenzie, J.L., "The Gospel According to Matthew," *Jerome Biblical Commentary*. Englewood Cliffs, N.J.: Prentice-Hall, 1968. II (pp. 69–71).

Mead, George H., *Mind, Self and Society*. Chicago: University of Chicago Press, 1934.

Mead, Margaret, *Cooperation and Competition Among Primitive Peoples*. New York: McGraw-Hill, 1937.

Mead, Sidney, *The Nation with the Soul of a Church*. New York: Harper and Row, 1975.

Medellín Documents. *The Church in the Present Day Transformation of Latin America in the Light of the Council*. Official English Edition. Washington, D.C.: United States Catholic Conference, and Bogota, Colombia: Latin American Episcopal Council, 1970.

Memmi, A., *The Colonizer and the Colonized*. Boston: Beacon Press, 1970.

Michels, Robert, *Political Parties*. New York: Collier, 1962.

Miguez-Bonino, Jose, *Doing Theology in a Revolutionary Situation*. Philadelphia: Fortress Press. 1975.

Mills, C. Wright, *The Sociological Imagination*. New York: Oxford University Press, 1959.

Montagu, Ashley (ed.)., *Sociobiology Examined*. New York: Oxford University Press, 1980.

Moore, Barrington, *Political Power and Social Theory*. New York: Harper and Row, 1962.

Moore, Barrington, *Social Origins of Dictatorship and Democracy*. Boston: Beacon Press, 1966.

Moore, Basil (ed.), *The Challenge of Black Theology in South Africa*. Atlanta, Georgia: John Knox Press, 1974.

Murphy, Elaine, *The Environment To Come: A Global Summary*. Washington, D.C.: Population Reference Bureau, 1983 (pamphlet).

Murphy, Elaine, *Food and Population: A Global Concern*, Washington, D.C.: Population Reference Bureau, 1984 (Pamphlet).

Murphy, Elaine, *World Population: Toward the Next Century*. Washington, D.C.: Population Reference Bureau, 1985 (Pamphlet).

Mzimela, Sipo E., *Apartheid: South African Naziism*. New York: Vantage Press, 1983.

National Federation of Priests' Councils, *Hear the Cries of Jerusalem*. Prepared for the National Federation of Priests' Councils by the Director of Ministry for Justice and Peace with the N.F.P.C. Justice and Peace Committee. National Federation of Priests' Councils, 1307 S. Wabash, Chicago, Illinois 60605.

National Opinion Research Center, *American Priests*. United States Catholic Conference, 1971.

Neal, Marie Augusta, *Values and Interests in Social Change*. Englewood Cliffs, N.J.: Prentice-Hall, 1965.

Neal, Marie Augusta, "Structural Implications of the CMSW Survey," Proceedings of the Annual Assembly, September 1967. Washington, D.C.: CMSW Secretariat, 1968.

Neal, Marie Augusta, "The Relation Between Religious Belief and Structural Change in Religious Orders," *Review of Religious Research*, Vol. XII, 1970. Part I, pp. 2–16; Part II, 1971, pp. 154–164.

Neal, Marie Augusta, *The Sociotheology of Letting Go: A First World Church Facing Third World People*. New York: Paulist Press, 1977.

Neal, Marie Augusta, "The Comparative Implications of Functional and Conflict Theory as Theoretical Frameworks for Religious Research and Religious Decision Making," *Review of Religious Research*, Vol. 21, No. 1, Fall 1979.

Neal, Marie Augusta, "The Challenge of Sociobiology," *Christianity and Crisis*, Vol. 40, No. 21, January 21, 1980a, pp. 342–349.

Neal, Marie Augusta, "Pathology of Women in a Man's Church," *Concilium* No. 134, edited by Virgil Elizondo and Norbert Greinacher, New York: Seabury Press, 1980.

Neal, Marie Augusta, *Catholic Sisters in Transition from the 1960s to the 1980s*. Wilmington, Delaware: Michael Glazier Inc., 1984.

Niebuhr, Reinhold, *Christianity and Power Politics*. New York: Charles Scribner's Sons, 1940.

Nossiter, Bernard D., "U.N. Study Predicts Slower Population Growth," *New York Times*, June 19, 1984, p. 19.

Novak, Michael, *Choosing Our King: Powerful Symbols in Presidential Politics*, New York: Macmillan, 1974.

Novak, Michael, *Toward a Theology of the Corporation*. Washington, D.C.: American Enterprise Institute for Public Policy Research, 1981.

Novak, Michael, "The Case against Liberation Theology," *New York Times Magazine*. October 21, 1984, pp. 51ff.

Novak, Michael et al, *Catholic Social Thought and the U.S. Economy* (A Lay Letter). New York: Lay Commission on Catholic Social Teaching and the U.S. Economy, 1984.

Nozick, Robert, *Anarchy, State and Utopia*. New York: Basic Books, 1975.

Ntwasa, Sabelo and B. Moore, "The Concept of God in Black Theology" in B. Moore (ed.), *The Challenge of Black Theology in South Africa*. Atlanta, Georgia: John Knox Press, 1974.

Nyerere, Julius, "Speech to the Maryknoll Sisters." Released by United Republic of Tanzania News Service (1978). Mission to the United Nations, 205 East 42nd Street, New York, New York.

O'Brien, David J. and Thomas A. Shannon, *Renewing the Earth, Catholic Documents on Peace, Justice and Liberation*. New York: Image, 1977.

O'Dea, Thomas, "Five Dilemmas in the Institutionalization of Religion," *Journal for the Scientific Study of Religion*, Vol. 1, 1961, pp. 30–41.

Otten, C. Michael, *Power, Values, and Society: An Introduction to Sociology*. Glenview, Illinois: Scott Foresman, 1981 (Now printed by Random House).

Oxford Annotated Bible. "Introduction to Isaiah," p. 882. New York: Oxford University Press, 1962.

Parsons, Talcott, *The System of Modern Society*. Englewood Cliffs, N.J.: Prentice Hall, 1971.

Paul VI, *Pastoral Constitution on the Church in the Modern World*. Boston: St. Paul Editions, 1965.

Paul VI, *A Call to Action*, Apostolic Letter on the Eightieth Anniversary of *Rerum Novarum*. Washington, D.C.: United States Catholic Conference, 1971.

Paul VI, *Apostolic Exhortation on Religious Life*. Official Vatican Translation of *Evangelica Testificatio*. Boston: Daughters of St. Paul, 1971.

Paul VI, *The Development of Peoples*. Creative translation by Father R.V. Bogan. Chicago: Claretian Publications, 1968, also in O'Brien and Shannon, pp. 313–345.

Peruvian Bishops, "Liberation Theology and the Gospel," *Origins*, Vol. 14, No. 31, January 17, 1985.

Pettigrew, Thomas and Ernest Campbell, *Christians in Racial Crisis*. Washington, D.C.: Public Affairs Press, 1959.

Pius XI, *On Reconstructing the Social Order* (*Quadragesimo Anno*) Washington, D.C.: National Catholic Welfare Conference, 1931.

Population Reference Bureau, "World Population Data Sheet." Population Reference Bureau, Inc., 1754 N. Street, N.W., Washington, D.C. 20036 (published annually).

Randall, Margaret, *Christians in the Nicaraguan Revolution*. Maryknoll, New York: Orbis, 1984.

Ratzinger, Joseph, "Instruction on Certain Aspects of the Theology of Liberation," *Origins*. Vol. 14, No. 13, September 13, 1984.

Rawls, John, *A Theory of Justice*. Cambridge, Massachusetts: Belknap Press, Harvard University, 1971.

Richard, Pablo et al., *Idols of Death and the God of Life*. Maryknoll, New York: Orbis, 1983.

Richey, Russell E. and Donald G. Jones, eds., *American Civil Religion*, New York: Harper and Row, 1974.

Ruether, Rosemary Radford, *Liberation Theology*. New York: Paulist Press, 1973.

Ruether, Rosemary Radford, ed., *Religion and Sexism: Images of Women in the Judeo-Christian Theological Tradition*. New York: Simon and Schuster, 1974.

Ruether, Rosemary Radford, *Sexism and Godtalk*. Boston: Beacon Press, 1983.

Rushton, J. Phillippe, *Altruism, Socialization, and Society*. Englewood Cliffs, New Jersey: Prentice-Hall, 1980.

Russell, Letty, *Human Liberation in a Feminist Perspective*. Philadelphia: Westminister Press, 1974.

Ryan, William, "Multinational Corporations and the New International Economic Order," *Church Alert* No. 16, 1977. Geneva. Switzerland: SODEPAX, pp. 2–8.

Schacter, S. *The Psychology of Affiliation*. Stanford: Stanford University Press, 1959.

Schiblin, Richard, *The Bible, the Church, and Social Justice*. Liguori, Missouri: Liguori Publications, 1983.

Schillebeeckx, E., "Liberation Theology between Medellín and Puebla," *Theology Digest*, Vol. 28, No. 1, Spring 1980, pp. 3–9.

Schnackenburg, R., *God's Rule and Kingdom*. Freiburg: Herder and Herder, 1963.

Segundo, Juan Luis. *The Community Called Church*. Maryknoll, New York: Orbis, 1973 (originally published 1968).

Select Commission on Immigration and Refugee Policy, "U.S. Immigration Policy and the National Interest" (Introduction by chairman Theodore M. Hesburgh, March 1, 1981).

Senior, Donald, C.P. and Carroll Stuhlmueller, C.P., *The Biblical Foundations for Mission*. Maryknoll, New York: Orbis, 1979.

Sisters of Notre Dame Pedagogy Project, *The Gospel Agenda in Global Perspective*, Research Paper No. 1. Boston: Emmanuel College, September 1981.

Sisters of Notre Dame Pedagogy Project, *Faith and Pedagogy: A Journey*. Research Paper No. 2, Boston: Emmanuel College, October 1984.

Sivard, Ruth Leger, *World Military and Social Expenditures, 1980*. Leesburg, Virginia: World Priorities, 1980. See also each annual issue.

Sklar, Holly, ed. *Trilateralism*. Boston: South End Press, 1980.

Sobrino, Jon, "Puebla: A Quiet Affirmation of Medellin," *Theology Digest*. Vol. 28, No. 1, Spring 1980, pp. 13–16.

Sobrino, Jon, *Christology at the Crossroads: A Latin American Approach* (tr. by John Drury). Maryknoll, New York: Orbis, 1978.

Sociobiology Study Group, "Sociobiology—A New Biological Determinism?" *Science for the People*, mimeographed, April, 1976.

SODEPAX, "Rocca di Papa Colliquium on the Social Thinking of the Churches," Parts I, II, III, IV. CHURCH ALERT, No. 17–20. Geneva, Switzerland: Ecumenical Center, 1977, 1978.

Soelle, Dorothee, *Political Theology*. Philadelphia: Fortress Press, 1974.

Solomon, Mark, *Death Waltz to Armageddon: E.P. Thompson and the Peace Movement*. New York: U.S. Peace Council, 1984 (Pamphlet).

Sorokin, Pitirim A., *The Crisis of Our Age*. New York: E.P. Dutton, 1941.

Sorokin, Pitirim A., *Man and Society in Calamity*. New York: E.P. Dutton, 1942.

Sorokin, Pitirim A., *The Reconstruction of Humanity*. Boston: Beacon Press, 1948.

Sorokin, Pitirim A., *Social and Cultural Dynamics*, 4 vols. New York: American Book Company, 1937, 1941.

Sorokin, Pitirim A., *Explorations in Altruistic Love and Behavior* (Symposium). Boston: Beacon Press, 1950a.

Sorokin, Pitirim A., *Society, Culture and Personality*. New York: Harper and Row, 1947.

Sorokin, Pitirim A., *Social Philosophies in an Age of Crisis*. Boston: Beacon Press, 1950b.

Sorokin, Pitirim A., "Factors of Altruism and Egoism," *Sociology and Social Research* xxxii, 675–678, 1948.

South African Institute of Race Relations, Interview with Father Cosmas Desmond. Johannesburg: South African Institute of Race Relations, 1970.

Stackhouse, Max L., "Some Intellectual and Social Roots of Modern Human Rights Ideas," *Journal for the Scientific Study of Religion*, 20, pp. 301–309.

Steidl-Meier, S.J. *Social Justice Ministry: Foundations and Concerns*. New York: Le Jacq Inc., 1984.

Suhard, Emmanuel Cardinal, *Growth or Decline: The Church Today*. South Bend, Indiana: Fides Publishers, 1948.

Sweezy, P. and C. Bettleheim, *On the Transition to Socialism*. New York: Monthly Review Press, 1971.

Synod of Bishops, *Synodal Document on Justice in the World*, Second General Assembly of Synod of Bishops, Rome, November 30, 1971. Boston: St. Paul Editions, 1971.

Tamez, Elsa, *The Bible of the Oppressed*. Maryknoll, New York: Orbis, 1982.

Task Force on Peace, "The National Budget and Reordering National Priorities, 1972," Prepared by Task Force on Peace, Catholic Committee on Urban Ministry, Box 606, Notre Dame, Indiana, 46556.

Third World Theologians, "Statement of the Ecumenical Dialogue of Third World Theologians," at Dar es Salaam, August 5–11, 1976, in Document No. 2, *Theology in the Americas* document series. New York, 1978 (mimeographed).

Torres, Sergio and John Eagleson, *Theology in the Americas*. Maryknoll, New York: Orbis, 1976.

Tucker, Robert C., ed., *The Marx-Engels Reader*. New York: W.W. Norton, 1972.

United Nations, "Declaration on the Establishment of a New International Economic Order," 9th plenary meeting, 1 May 1974. New York: United Nations Information Office, 1974.

United Nations, *Charter of Economic Rights and Duties of States.* United Nations Office of Public Education, February 1975.

United Nations, *The International Covenants on Human Rights and Optional Protocol.* United Nations Information Center, 1976. (This document was later published as the United Nations Bill of Rights, 1978.)

United Nations, *Toward a World Economy That Works.* New York: United Nations Information Office, 1980.

United States Catholic Conference. "The Challenge of Peace: God's Promise and Our Response." *Origins,* May 19, 1983, Vol. 13, No. 1.

United States Catholic Conference. "Catholic Social Teaching and the United States Economy," first draft—bishops' pastoral on the economy. *Origins,* November 15, 1984, Vol. 14, No. 22/23.

Urban Bishops Coalition, *To Hear and To Heed: The Episcopal Church Listens and Acts in the City.* Cincinnati: Forward Movement Publications, 1978.

Van de Berghe, Pierre L., *South Africa: A Study in Conflict.* Los Angeles: University of California Press, 1967.

Van de Berghe, Pierre L., *Man in Society: a Biosocial View.* New York: Elsevier, 1978.

Vandermeer, John. "Hardin's Lifeboat Adrift," *Science for the People,* January 1976, pp. 16–19.

Varacalli, Joseph A., *Toward the Establishment of Liberal Catholicism in America.* Washington, D.C.: University Press of America, 1983.

Vawter, Bruce, "Introduction to Prophetic Literature," *Jerome Biblical Commentary.* Englewood Cliffs: Prentice-Hall, 1968, I (pp. 223–229).

Vaz, de Lima, H., "The Church and Conscientizacao," *America,* 1968, Vol. 118, pp. 578–580.

Von Rad, G., *The Message of the Prophets.* New York: Harper and Row, 1962.

Walsh, Michael and Brian Davies, eds. *Proclaiming Justice and*

Peace: Documents from John XXIII-John Paul II, Mystic Connecticut: Twenty-Third Publications, 1984.

Weber, Max, *Theory of Social and Economic Organization*, ed. by Talcott Parsons. New York: Oxford University Press, 1937, pp. 328–345.

Weber, Max, *The Protestant Ethic and the Spirit of Capitalism*. New York: Charles Scribner's Sons, 1958.

Weber, Max, *Sociology of Religion*. Boston: Beacon Press, 1963 (originally published 1922).

Webster, Douglas. "The Debate on Social Sin Continues," *The Ecumenist*, Vol. 22, No. 2, Jan./Feb. 1984.

Wilson, Edward O., *The Insect Societies*. Harvard University Press, 1971.

Wilson, Edward O., *Sociobiology: The New Synthesis*. Cambridge, Massachusetts: Harvard University Press, 1975.

Wilson, Edward O., *On Human Nature*. Cambridge, Massachusetts: Harvard University Press, 1978a.

Wilson, Edward O., "What Is Sociobiology?" *Society*, Vol. 16, No. 6, Sept/Oct. 1978b. pp. 10–14.

Wilson, Edward O., "Altruism," *Harvard Magazine*, Nov/Dec. 1978c, pp. 23–28.

Wilson, Edward O., *Genes, Mind and Culture*. Cambridge, Massachusetts: Harvard University Press, 1981.

Winter, Gibson, *The Suburban Captivity of the Churches: An Analysis of Protestant Responsibility in the Expanding Metropolis*. New York: Doubleday, 1961.

Wispe, Lauren (ed.), *Altruism, Sympathy and Helping: Psychological and Sociological Principles*. New York: Academic Press, 1978.

Wolcott, Roger T., "Church and Social Action: Steelworkers and Bishops in Youngstown," *Journal for the Scientific Study of Religion*, 21, pp. 71–79.

World Bank, *World Development Report, 1980*. Washington, D.C.: World Bank, 1980.

World Resource Institute, *The Global Possible: Resources Development in the New Century*. Washington, D.C., 1984.

Wuthnow, Robert, *The Consciousness Reformation*. Berkeley: University of California Press, 1976.

Wuthnow, Robert. "Two Traditions of Religious Studies," *Journal for the Scientific Study of Religion*, Vol. 20, No. 1, March 1981, pp. 16–32.

Zorbaugh, Harvey, *The Gold Coast and the Slum*. Chicago: University of Chicago Press, 1929.

Notes

I. A Gospel Mandate

1. Population Data Sheet, *Population Reference Bureau*, Washington, D.C., 1980, 1981.

II. The Prophetic Tradition

1. The prophetic nature of *Call to Action* may be appreciated by contrast to the 1868 Vatican decrees forbidding Italian Catholics from participating in parliamentary elections. Pope Pius IX initiated this policy during a period of uncertainty after the promulgation of the Constitution of the kingdom of Italy (1861). Apart from concern that the oath taken by deputies might be interpreted as approval of the spoliation of the Holy See, the Pope was also prompted in *Non Expedit* by a belief that "the masses seemed unprepared for parliamentary government." U. Benigni, *Catholic Encyclopedia* XI (New York: Encyclopedia Press, 1911), pp. 98–99.

2. In striking parallel to this Brazilian analysis, 101 South African churchmen in 1985 published "The Kairos Document" in which they described three theologies that characterize their country. The first, a "state theology," appeals to Romans 13:1–7 where Paul says we should obey the state. This they cannot do now that the state, through apartheid, is unjust. The second, a "church theology," stresses reconciliation, peace, justice and non-violence. Right now this is inadequate, irrelevant, and in-

effective because apartheid is the law. The third, a prophetic theology, based on a reading of the signs of the times, a social analysis of the conflicting forces of interests, takes a clear stand in the crisis. God sides with the oppressed.

III. Toward a New Civil Religion

1. The concept of sociobiology will be discussed at length later in this chapter. See Wilson, 1978.

2. See the writings of Garrett Hardin, including "The Tragedy of the Commons," *Science* 162 (December 1968); "Living on a Lifeboat," *Bioscience* 24 (October 1974): 561–68; "Where the Thinking Heart Beats the Bleeding Heart," *Boston Globe,* July 14, 1979, p. 11. Contrast Geoffrey Barraclough, "Wealth and Power: The Politics of Food and Oil," *New York Review of Books,* August 7, 1975; Frances M. Lappé and Joseph Collins, *Food First: Beyond the Myth of Scarcity,* (Boston: Houghton Mifflin, 1977); Richard J. Barnett and Ronald E. Miller, *Global Reach: The Power of the Multi-National Corporations* (New York: Simon and Schuster, 1974).

The author has pursued these issues at greater length elsewhere. See "A Turning Point of Religious Ethics," *The Ecumenist* 46 (November–December 1977); "Sociobiology," book review in *Sociological Analysis* 39 (Summer 1978); "Civil Religion," *New Catholic Encyclopedia* 17 (1979); "Civil Religion and the Development of Peoples," *Religious Education Review* 22 (May–June 1976).

3. See *New York Times'* account of Secretary of Agriculture John R. Block's message to American farmers, July 11, 1982, p. 16. In 1974, the third world nations sponsored the Sixth General Assembly of the United Nations to make their case for presence at decisions for trade and aid. That proposal for a New International Economic Order received affirmation from 131 nations but not from those who determine the decisions. Six nations opposed it, the United States included. We have scarcely begun examining the potential for international control embodied in the convergence of telecommunications and computer technologies, especially the effect this powerful combination will have on the destinies of poorer peoples. See Cerni, 1984.

4. This section is taken, with minor changes, from my "Civil Religion," *New Catholic Encyclopedia* 17 (1979).

5. Jean Jacques Rousseau, *The Social Contract and Discourses*, trans. G. Cole (New York: Dutton, 1950), pp. 129–41.

6. Robert N. Bellah, "Civil Religion in America," *Daedalus* (Winter 1967), reprinted in *American Civil Religion*, ed. Russel E. Richey and Donald G. Jones (New York: Harper and Row, 1974), p. 21.

7. Ibid., p. 33.

8. Authority, that is, the right to use power, is a major concept in sociological analysis. Weber traces three bases on which authority is effective: charisma, tradition, law (Weber, *The Theory of Social and Economic Organization*, pp. 333f).

9. Robert N. Bellah, *The Broken Covenant* (New York: Seabury Press, 1975), p. 139.

10. See Philip E. Hammond, "Sociology of American Civil Religion," *Sociological Analysis* 37 (Summer 1976), 127–39; Richard Fenn, "Bellah and the New Orthodoxy," *Sociological Analysis* 37, 160–67. See also *Religious Education* (May–June 1976); Fenn, 1978; Gehrig, 1981.

11. See Gregory Baum, *Religion and Alienation* (New York: Paulist Press, 1975); Sr. Marie Augusta Neal, *A Socio-Theology of Letting-Go* (New York: Paulist Press, 1977); José Comblin, *The Church and the National Security State* (New York: Orbis Books, 1979).

12. Compare Michael Novak, *Choosing Our King: Powerful Symbols in Presidential Politics* (New York: Macmillan, 1974) and Marie Augusta Neal, "Civil Religion and the Development of Peoples," *Religious Education* (May–June 1976): 244–60.

13. See Peter L. Berger, *The Sacred Canopy* (Garden City, N.Y.: Doubleday, 1969) for the beginning of this theme that continues throughout his writings in the 1970's.

14. See Alessandro Cussianovich, *Religious Life and the Poor: A Liberation Theology Perspective* (New York: Paulist Press, 1979). Contrast Robert N. Bellah and Charles Glock, eds., *New Religious Consciousness* (Berkeley, California: University of California, 1977).

15. The sociobiology debate has centered on Edward O. Wilson's *Sociobiology: A New Synthesis* (Cambridge, Mass.: Harvard University Press, 1975) and his later *On Human Nature* (Cambridge, Mass.: Harvard University Press, 1978a). For the debate, see Arthur L. Caplan, *The Sociobiology Debate: Readings in Ethical and Scientific Issues* (New York: Harper and Row, 1978). See the journal devoted to the field, *The Journal of Social and Biological Structure: Studies in Human Sociobiology,* ed. Harry Wheeler and James P. Danielli (New York: Academic Press, 1976). Psychology and sociology textbooks in paperback and hardcover editions are already on the market. See David P. Barash, *Sociobiology and Behavior* (New York: Elsevier, 1977), my review of this book in *Sociological Analysis* 39 (Summer 1978): 185–187, and Pierre L. Van der Berghe, *Man and Society* (New York: Elsevier, 1978), the latter an introductory sociology text. These three authors recognize one another's contributions. See also Michael S. Gregory, Anita Silvers and Diane Sutch, eds., *Sociobiology and Human Nature: An Interdisciplinary Critique and Defense* (San Francisco: Jossey-Bass, 1978). *Time Magazine* recognized the field with its cover story on August 1, 1977. The 1978 annual meeting of the American Association for the Advancement of Science devoted two days of its program to the topic. Wilson and Hardin have received National Medal of Science awards from the U.S. President and acclaim from AAAS. To hear Wilson speaking across the disciplines, see his "Biology and the Social Sciences," *Daedalus* 2 (Fall 1977): 127–39. See also the entire issue of *Society* 15 (September–October 1978).

16. Wilson, *On Human Nature,* pp. 165, 193.

17. Edward O. Wilson, "Altruism," *Harvard Magazine* (November–December 1978): 23–78; *Sociobiology,* chs. 1, 5, and 27; *On Human Nature,* chs. 7, 8, and 9, esp. pp. 199, 189, also pp. 177–192, 205–07. See also Stuart Hampshire's review, "The Illusion of Sociobiology," *New York Review of Books,* October 12, 1978.

18. For a review and summary of these church documents, see "Rocca di Papa Colloquium on the Social Thinking of the Churches," *Church Alert,* pts. 1, 2, 3, 4, nos. 17–20.

19. See Wilson, *On Human Nature,* p. 192 and Van der Berghe,

Man and Society, pp. 60, 170, 99–100, in that order. *Man and Society* (second ed.) should be read *in toto* to see this problem manifest. The critical factor has to do with the evidence. Wilson and Baruch admit there is none. Van der Berghe claims the other two have provided it. All admit that systematic observation of primate behavior is less than two decades old (Van der Berghe, p. 27). Yet, given that fragile basis of plausibility, the discipline has invaded the classrooms of human psychology, sociology, and anthropology at every grade level. Why this popularity for a thesis so in keeping with a public policy regarding outsiders and the uses of aggression?

20. *The United Nations' Covenants on Human Rights* (New York: United Nations Information Center, 1976).

21. See *The Church and Human Rights* (Vatican City: Pontifical Commission on Justice and Peace, 1975), and *Church Alert*, nos. 16–18 (Geneva: SODEPAX, World Council of Churches, 1977–78). See Sodepax in Bibliography.

22. See William Ryan, "Multinational Corporations and the New International Economic Order," *Church Alert* 16 (1977); "Evangelization—A Political Problem?" *Pro Mundi Vita* 38 (1975). See also Evans and Evans, 1983; Dorr, 1983.

23. For a discussion and bibliography on liberation theology, see Gustavo Gutiérrez, *Theology of Liberation* (Maryknoll, N.Y.: Orbis Books, 1971); Robert McAfee Brown, *Theology in a New Key* (Philadelphia: Westminster Press, 1978); Dorothee Soelle, *Political Theology* (Philadelphia: Fortress Press, 1974). See also the recent general listings of Orbis Books, Maryknoll, N.Y., 1986. See also *Origins*.

24. This was particularly evident in the reporting of the 1976 "Call to Action" Conference, a national convocation of the Catholic Church in Detroit. One hundred and sixty decisions were taken, dealing mainly with action for the renewal of life for people in exploitative situations, including the cities, Appalachia, and farm workers. The media, however, focused on concern for a married clergy, divorced Catholics, and women priests—all important issues, but not the conference's main agenda.

VI. The Future of Altruism

1. These data have been circulated by the Population Reference Bureau, Washington, D.C., annually since 1960. Most of them come from United Nations sources. The projections are reported by Dr. T.N. Krishnan, a senior consultant with the United Nations Fund for Populations Activities, *New York Times*, June 15, 1981.

2. The twenty-four developed, market-economy countries include Australia, Austria, Belgium, Canada, Denmark, Finland, France, Germany (Federal Republic), Greece, Iceland, Ireland, Italy, Japan, Luxembourg, Netherlands, New Zealand, Norway, Portugal, Spain, Sweden, Switzerland, Turkey, United Kingdom, United States. The nine centrally-planned economies include Albania, Bulgaria, Czechoslovakia, German Democratic Republic, Hungary, Mongolia, Poland, Romania, USSR (United Nations, *A World Economy That Works*, 1980).

3. These data appear on the World Population Data Sheet for 1981 issued by the Population Reference Bureau. "More developed" refers to Europe, North America, Australia, New Zealand, Japan and the USSR.

4. This index appears on the 1979 Population Data Sheet of the Population Reference Bureau. It was developed by the Overseas Development Council, Washington, D.C.

5. The United Nations Bill of Rights is the development of the Declaration on Human Rights of 1948 elaborated into a treaty. It is made up of three documents: The Covenant on Civil and Political Rights, the Covenant on Economic, Social and Cultural Rights, and the Optional Protocol to the Covenant on Civil and Political Rights. A country ratifying the first covenant undertakes to protect its people by law against cruel, inhuman or degrading treatment. It recognizes the right of every human being to life, liberty, security, and privacy of person. The covenant prohibits slavery, guarantees the right to a fair trial and protects persons against arbitrary arrest or detention. It recognizes freedom of thought, conscience and religion, freedom of opinion and expression, the right of peaceful assembly and

of emigration, and freedom of association. A country ratifying the second covenant—on economic, social and cultural rights—acknowledges its responsibility to promote better living conditions for its people. It recognizes everyone's right to work, to fair wages, to social security, to adequate standards of living and freedom from hunger, and to health and education. It also undertakes to assure the right of everyone to form and join trade unions. Both covenants recognize the rights of all people to self-determination and to enjoy and utilize fully and freely their natural wealth and resources. The Optional Protocol enables the Human Rights Committee of the United Nations to consider communications from private individuals claiming to be victims of a state which is party to the protocol. Some nations have signed one or the other of the two basic covenants; over fifty nations have signed both. Since they are treaties, they require U.S. Senate action in this country, an action that has not yet been initiated (United Nations, 1978, p. 2).

6. Compare Garrett Hardin's "Tragedy of the Commons," *Science* (1968) with *U.S. Immigration Policy and the National Interest: Executive Summary of the Final Report and Recommendations of the Select Commission on Immigration and Refugee Policy*, with an introduction by Chairman Theodore M. Hesburgh, March 1, 1981 (Washington, D.C.: U.S. Printing Office).

7. See *World Military and Social Expenditures*, by Ruth Leger Sivard, 1980 and following years. An annual series on world priorities, this issue highlights nuclear risk. It compares military expenditures with corresponding national expenditures on education, health, nutrition and water.

8. A landmark volume published in 1965 and having no chapter on altruism is Bernard Siedenberg, *Basic Studies in Social Psychology* (New York: Holt, Rinehart and Winston, 1965).

9. The sociobiology debate set off by the Wilson publication began in the *New York Review of Books* and then, after publication of his *On Human Nature* (Harvard, 1978), moved to several publications themselves preceded by scholarly forums. See Michael S. Gregory, Anita Silvers, Diane Sutch (eds.), *Sociobiology and Human Nature* (Jossey Bass, 1978); Arthur L. Caplan (ed.), *The Sociobiology Debate: Readings on Ethical and*

Scientific Issues (New York: Harper and Row, 1978). In 1980, Ashley Montagu edited *Sociobiology Examined,* a critical volume in which fifteen different perspectives and disciplines questioned the Wilson enterprise (Oxford University Press). Montagu cited the research of Nicholas Pastor, *The Nature-Nurture Controversy* (New York: King's Crown Press, 1949) to substantiate this observation.

10. Some of the better-known liberation theologians writing from the Latin American experience include Gustavo Gutiérrez, José Comblin, Juan Luis Segundo, Jon Sobrino, M. Míguez-Bonino. Paolo Freire is a Brazilian educator whose method of teaching literacy in the villages and *favelas* incorporates a reflection on the gospel out of which emerges a liberation theology, in an action-reflection model. The involvement of the wider church in this justice action is recounted in detail in *Church Alert* Nos. 17–20 (Geneva: SODEPAX, 1977–78).

V. Altruism as Public Virtue

1. This account appeared in the *New York Times,* May 10, 1982 in a report by Charles Austin, p. B6.

2. Orbis Books is publishing a volume on pedagogies for the non-poor in 1986, edited by Robert and Alice Evans.

3. This is a formulation from the constitutions of the Sisters of Notre Dame de Namur. It appears in the National Sisters' Survey of 1980, sponsored by the Leadership Conference of Women Religious as Item 395 and is agreed to by 83 percent of the 3,740 sisters responding, a random sample of twenty selected congregations.

4. See "World Could Reach Ultimate Population of 10 Billion People," by Mary Barberis, in *Intercom: International Population News Magazine,* Population Reference Bureau, Washington, D.C., Vol. 8, no. 4 (April 1980), p. 1. The *New York Times* reports: "U.N. Predicts World Population Will Level at 10.5 Billion in 2110," by Alan Cowell, June 15, 1981, p. 4; "U.N. Lowers Estimates of Population in 2000," June 13, 1982, p. 4; "U.N. Study Predicts Slower Population Gains," by Bernard D. Nossiter, June 19, 1983, p. 4.

VI. Social Justice and the Right to Use Power

1. See *The Sacred in a Post-Secular Age,* edited by Philip Hammond (University of California Press, 1985).

2. See *Rerum Novarum,* the first of a series of encyclical letters published by the Catholic Church and dealing with the rights of workers to a fair share of the profits of industry by reason of their personhood. See also *Quadragesimo Anno,* 1931; *Mater et Magistra,* 1961; *Octogesimo Anno,* 1971; *Laborem Exercens,* 1981 (Boston: St. Paul Editions).

3. Given the current discussion of ownership, the remainder of the Thomas Aquinas quotation is significant. It reads: "Nevertheless, if the need be so manifest and urgent that it is evident that the present need must be remedied by whatever means is at hand (for instance, when a person is in some imminent danger and there is no other possible remedy), then it is lawful for a man to succor his own need by means of another's property, by taking it openly or secretly: nor is this properly speaking theft or robbery" (*Summa Theologica,* II, II, q. 66, A. 7; see also Avila, *Ownership*).

VII. Education for Justice

1. W.I. Thomas formulated this thesis in the early 1920's: "If people define a situation as real, it is real in its consequences." Later this proposition was included in theory in symbolic interaction. See Herbert Blumer's *Symbolic Interactionism: Perspective and Method* (Englewood Cliffs, New Jersey: Prentice-Hall, 1969, pp. 117–126).

IX. A Socio-Theology of Relinquishment

1. Data on population and related GNP are available from the Population Reference Bureau, 2213 M St., N.W., Washington, D.C. 20037. Annual Population Data Sheets update these data and provide useful charts for teaching purposes.

2. It is important to note that what some see as potentially

hopeful in population and food predictions, others still see as a great danger because of failure to plan. See *Intercom*, the international population news magazine (March–April 1983), for a cautious interpretation, and Murphy (1984) for a more optimistic one. Both reports come from the same organization, the Population Reference Bureau. Roger Ravelle, of the Harvard University Population Center, made this high calculation in 1972. His colleague in the same center, Nathan Kayfitz, made a low estimate of six billion as the upper limit of world carrying capacity.

3. The Center of Concern in Washington, D.C. and Network, an organization founded by Catholic Sisters and now expanded to provide political education on social justice issues, both provide workshops on the encyclicals as they develop a foundation for social justice education.